TALKING OUT OF ALCOHOLISM

Talking out of Alcoholism

THE SELF-HELP PROCESS OF ALCOHOLICS ANONYMOUS

DAVID ROBINSON

UNIVERSITY PARK PRESS BALTIMORE

054639

© 1979 David Robinson
Published in North America by
UNIVERSITY PARK PRESS
233 East Redwood Street
Baltimore, Maryland

Library of Congress Cataloging in Publication Data

Robinson, David, 1941-
    Talking out of alcoholism.

    Includes bibliographical references and indexes.
    1.   Alcoholics Anonymous   2.   Alcoholism —
Treatment.   I.   Title.
HV5278.R6   1979   362.2'92   78-20506
ISBN 0-8391-1371-4

Printed and bound in Great Britain

CONTENTS

ACKNOWLEDGEMENTS

In relation to a book like this there are many people whose help is gratefully acknowledged: Griffith Edwards for his guidance and interest in this piece of work which builds on his own previous studies of AA; the Department of Health and Social Security and the Medical Research Council for their financial support; Colin Taylor for his statistical advice and Ruby Bendall for her involvement at all stages from the initial discussions about the survey via coding and extracting material from the schedules to the typing of the final manuscript.

Stuart Henry worked extremely energetically on the project until the preliminary analysis had been completed. While, unfortunately, I cannot hold him responsible for the shortcomings of this book he knows the degree to which any virtues it may have stem directly from our close collaboration during his time at the Addiction Research Unit.

My main debt of gratitude, of course, is to Alcoholics Anonymous. Bill and his colleagues at the General Service Office in Redcliffe Gardens were invaluable helpers, not only with the technicalities of administering the survey but with their comments about the schedules and their openness about the workings of the organisation. But, as Bill would be first to acknowledge, this book could not have been written just from 'Head Office'. It depended upon the generous willingness of very many group members to be interviewed, tape-recorded, watched, written to, telephoned and otherwise pestered in our attempt to describe the who, what, when and where of the fellowship and to unravel the self-help process of talking out of alcoholism.

Addiction Research Unit   David Robinson
Institute of Psychiatry
London
31 December 1978

INTRODUCTION

> AA merits more understanding than the current state of
> knowledge about it affords. (Leach 1973)

Alcoholics Anonymous is a widely respected response to one of the
major health and social problems of our time. The consumption of
alcohol has been implicated as a significant contributory factor not only
in a whole range of physical and mental illnesses, but also in divorce,
desertion and family disintegration; in household, work and traffic
accidents; in violence, murder and suicide; and in loss of jobs and
destitution: in short, in almost every situation in which harm is done by
people to themselves or to others.

From its inception in 1935, Alcoholics Anonymous has grown into a
worldwide organisation claiming well over 1,000,000 active members.
Not only has its growth been rapid, but the praise which has been given
to AA has been lavish. R.G. McCarthy, one of the pioneers of alcohol
studies suggested as early as 1946 that 'the remarkable success' of
Alcoholics Anonymous has been 'perhaps without parallel in our
society', while twenty years later the editors of a special volume of the
Annals of the New York Academy of Sciences (1974) declared that 'the
success of AA in helping alcoholics to achieve a continued sobriety
has been one of the major phenomena of the century'.

It is not just scientific experts and professionals involved with the
treatment of alcoholism who feel that AA has something special to
offer. A general population survey conducted in South London (Robinson
1976) revealed that of all the routine helping organisations and professions, Alcoholics Anonymous was considered to be the most useful
'for someone whose drinking is causing them problems', while Mowrer
(1961) felt that Alcoholics Anonymous exemplified a method and
philosophy that held out a significant hope for the future of mankind:

> The trail which AA has blazed is the only one down which I can at
> present gaze and see anything that looks like a road to the future.
> How AA principles can be adapted or modified to meet the needs of
> other kinds of confused and suffering people is not fully clear to me.
> But I am as sure as I can be of anything that no therapy will be
> radically and broadly successful which does not take the neurotic's
> guilt seriously and does not help him admit his errors openly and

find ways to work in dead earnest to rectify and compensate for them.

Despite the widespread expert, professional and lay belief in its impressive record of success, Alcoholics Anonymous has been surprisingly little studied. There have been very few attempts even to find out who goes to AA, when and where. In the United Kingdom, apart from Edwards's (1967) survey of London groups and a small unpublished survey by the General Service Board of AA (1972a), we have very little basic descriptive material on this highly regarded organisation. Until very recently there has been no serious attempt to document or verify the extent of AA's success in comparison with other systems of help or even in its own terms. Leach (1973), under the heading *Does Alcoholics Anonymous Really Work?* draws on a small number of available studies plus the AA General Service Board Survey of members in the United States and Canada and concludes that 'Yes, Alcoholics Anonymous really does work'. But even if we accept Leach's conclusion, which Bebbington (1976) and others suggest we should not, there are related and no less important questions to be considered, such as for whom does AA 'really work', and *how*?

In an attempt to answer this last question we conducted a national survey of AA in November 1976 in co-operation with the General Service Office in London. Detailed self-completion questionnaires (see Appendix) were given to one in four members attending the meetings of a one in ten sample of the groups then operating in England and Wales and dealt not only with many aspects of AA organisation, structure and philosophy but also with members' personal histories, activities in the fellowship and attitudes toward it. The one hundred and seventy-one questionnaires which were completed and returned represented a response rate of 85.4 per cent. The sample survey, however, was only one part of the study of AA. In addition, members were extensively interviewed in their homes; group meetings were regularly attended and, in some cases, taped; the literature about and produced by AA was analysed; and a series of patients at the Maudsley hospital outpatient alcoholism clinic were interviewed to get some idea of why non-AAs had never been to the fellowship and why ex-AAs had left.

Alcoholics Anonymous is of interest, however, not merely in the context of alcoholism treatment, but also because of the place it occupies in the self-help movement. It is clear that the relationships between professionals, the public and governments are changing. Money is in short supply and in many countries the range and scale of professional health and social services are being refocused, reorganised and generally rethought. Closely allied to these shifts has been the rapid and substantial growth of self-help groups and organisations which, taken together, now represent a significant feature of contemporary life (Robinson and Henry 1977). As well as the familiar groups like Gamblers Anonymous, and Gingerbread, there are groups for the mentally ill, the physically handicapped, for people who eat too much and for those who refuse to eat at all, for the old and for the young, for stutterers and little people, for the blind and the deaf, the worried, the frightened, the lonely and for hundreds more besides, including the delightful, but as yet unconfirmed, Analysands Anonymous (Hurvitz 1970) open to anyone who has been in analysis for twelve years or more and who needs a power greater than their own or that of their analyst to terminate the analysis.

As well as the main-stream of self-help groups in which people with similar problems come together for mutual aid and support, there are other related developments which are often referred to as part of the self-help movement. Among them are the various volunteer schemes, the many 'integrity' and other small groups which aim to re-create primary group living in an attempt to compensate for what is seen as the disintegration of home, church and neighbourhood in the latter part of the twentieth century, the growing number of self-treatment groups, self-examination and self-care programmes which aim, among other things, to lessen the individual's dependence on medical and other helping professionals and, finally, the 'health by the people' (Newell 1975) and other self-help developments which are beginning to play such a crucial part in the structure of primary health care in developing countries.

Alcoholics Anonymous occupies an important place in the literature and practice of the modern self-help movement, not only because of its rapid growth into an international organisation but because it is so articulate about its activities and so unashamedly used as a model by many of the newer self-help groups. In many cases, however, the newer groups 'copy' from an outdated, unrealistic or just plain incorrect picture of what they imagine Alcoholics Anonymous to be. Similarly, medical and other professionals who refer or try to persuade patients and clients to go to AA do so with only the flimsiest idea of what is involved in being a member of AA and what the newcomer can expect. The aim of this book is to present, on the basis of the available literature, observations and a national survey of members, a realistic picture of the self-help process of Alcoholics Anonymous.

Chapter 1, 'Alcoholics Anonymous', traces the history of AA from its origins in Ohio in 1935 via its introduction into England to its current position as an important international organisation. The rate of growth is discussed, together with questions of 'success', organisation, finance and membership. The final section reviews various interpretations of AA and places the programme of recovery firmly within the framework of self-help.

Chapter 2, 'Becoming a Member', deals first of all with the question of affiliation and how people get to know about AA, come to settle on alcoholism as 'the' problem and come to be 'twelfth stepped' by an AA member. From listening to members' experiences, meeting a range of members at several different AA meetings, and reading the literature, the newcomer is gradually learning to 'identify' with the fellowship and become a member. Not everyone who has some kind of alcohol-related problem goes to AA, of course, and many of those who do go 'drop out'. Both these key issues are discussed.

Chapter 3, 'Sharing the Problem', shows how the fellowship deals not merely with drinking problems but with the whole range of problems with which the member is faced; from problems of stigma and problems with relationships, to practical difficulties of everyday living. But in spite of handling this wide range of problems members are encouraged to focus on the 'simple', straightforward problem of not drinking. This is managed through the use of AA literature and group support in the context of knowledge, example and 'shared' experiences and the programme message is carried in the talks and stories which are at the heart of the self-help process of AA.

Chapter 4, 'Coping through Involvement', emphasises that the self-help process of Alcoholics Anonymous involves more than mutual support, identification, and shared experiences. Although these are vital, they need, in most cases, to be supplemented by action. Action is encouraged, structured around projects, assessed in relation to time in the fellowship, and involves attendance at meetings, sponsorship and twelfth stepping, office holding, attending AA events, representing AA to other organisations and much more besides. Sobriety, the goal of Alcoholics Anonymous, is achieved not merely by not doing something − not drinking − but by doing something − being continuously 'involved'.

Chapter 5, 'AA as a Way of Life', discusses the crucial point that being an AA member does not just mean being involved in AA activities. The self-help process of AA involves forming friendships and other relationships through which the AA method is carried over into everyday

life. Meeting other AAs at home, at work and on social occasions
ensures the vital continuity of help which no professional can provide.
Help is always available rather than having to be sought, while the
processes of problem solving which have been learnt in the fellowship
can be applied to any of the everyday problems of living with which the
member is faced. For some people it is the method rather than the
meetings which becomes a way of life, and so these people grow out of,
rather than drop out of, the fellowship. The chapter also highlights
certain changes that members would like to see in the way the fellowship
operates, particularly in relation to its policy on publicity and
anonymity.

It is hoped that this picture of Alcoholics Anonymous will enable
those who have some alcohol-related problem to make more rational
decisions about whether AA has something to offer to them. In addition,
it is hoped that the book will be of interest and value to those many
professionals; psychiatrists, social workers, general practitioners and
others, who talk so readily about AA, who advise their patients and
clients to go to AA, and yet who know so little about Alcoholics
Anonymous and how it works.

1 ALCOHOLICS ANONYMOUS

> Alcoholics Anonymous is a fellowship of men and women who
> share their experience, strength and hope with each other that
> they may solve their common problem and help others to
> recover from alcoholism. (The AA Preamble)

Two major themes run through most of the accounts of why self-help
groups are flourishing today: disillusionment with existing helping
services and the decline of supportive social institutions. In explaining
the growth and development of the self-help movement, commentators
have given a great deal of emphasis to the widespread disillusionment
with the professions in general and the medical profession in particular.
Several commentators have seen the emergence of consumer-initiated
services as a response to the gap between the needs that people feel and
the existence of available services, facilities or social benefits to meet
such needs. At a more specific level, the medical correspondent of the
Sunday Times (Gillie 1975) felt that people who expect doctors to solve
their problems are disappointed

> . . . because the average over-worked GP might have neither the time
> nor the knowledge to [do so]. . . . The people who miss out are those
> with a genuine problem which the doctor does not recognise and
> many more whose problems are as much social as medical. Today
> these gaps in the health and social services are being plugged by
> dozens of voluntary and self-help organisations.

Linked to this disillusionment with the existing services is an increasingly articulate anti-professionalism. There is a growing realisation
that professionals have no answer to the great majority of everyday
problems of living and, furthermore, that the one-to-one relationship
between professional and client is not merely uneconomic but liable to
produce a stultifying dependence in the person who seeks help. Back
and Taylor (1976), for instance, see distrust of professionals as one of
the most striking characteristics of self-help supporters. They point out
that the easiest way of being accepted as one of the 'in' group is to
make a few slurring remarks about the doctors or social workers.

Disillusionment with the established helping services, anti-
professionalism, changing ideas about what medicine is or can do, a

decline in the traditional systems of social support and rejection of an over-individualistic and pragmatic world are some of the reasons given for the emergence of self-help. Katz and Bender (1976) include many of the reasons in their answer to the question, 'Why self-help?'

Industrialization, a money economy, the growth of vast structures of business, industry, government — all these have led to familiar specters the de-personalization and de-humanization of institutions and social life; feelings of alienation; powerlessness; the sense for many people that they are unable to control the events that shape their lives; the loss of choices; feelings of being trapped by impersonal forces; the decline of the sense of community, of identity. These problems are compounded for many by the loss of belief — in the church, the state, progress, politics and political parties, many established institutions and values. These same conditions give rise to many of the important social movements of the day — nationalism and ethnic consciousness, the civil rights struggles, Women's Liberation — all of which countertrend against the de-humanization and atomization, the discrimination and lack of nurturance in social institutions.

These broad themes underpinning the growth of the modern self-help movement are all important (Robinson and Henry 1977). No particular self-help group can start, however, without someone recognising that those who share a certain problem or condition, or set of circumstances can actually benefit from being in contact with each other. Further than that, of course, someone has to act on that recognition.

History and Growth

Of all self-help groups, Alcoholics Anonymous has perhaps the most well-developed written history. According to *Alcoholics Anonymous* (1939) and *Alcoholics Anonymous Comes of Age* (1957) AA originated in the chance meeting in Akron, Ohio, in the summer of 1935 between Robert Holbrook Smith, a local doctor, and a New York stockbroker called William Wilson. A year earlier, in 1934, Bill W. had been introduced to the Oxford religious groups by a friend who said that he was staying sober by attending their meetings and following their precepts. Impressed by his efforts, Bill W. attended some meetings and after what he termed 'a spiritual awakening' found that he also was able to remain sober. However, he failed to convert other alcoholics because of what his doctor, Dr William D. Silkworth, called 'too much preaching'.

Prior to his journey to Akron, the broker had worked hard with many alcoholics on the theory that only an alcoholic could help an alcoholic, but he had succeeded only in keeping sober himself. The broker had gone to Akron on a business venture which had collapsed, leaving him greatly in fear that he might start drinking again. He suddenly realized that in order to save himself he must carry his message to another alcoholic. That alcoholic turned out to be the Akron physician.

This physician had repeatedly tried spiritual means to resolve his alcoholic dilemma but had failed. But when the broker gave him Dr Silkworth's description of alcoholism and its hopelessness, the physician began to pursue the spiritual remedy for his malady with a willingness he had never before been able to muster. He sobered, never to drink again up to the moment of his death in 1950. This seemed to prove that one alcoholic could affect another as no non-alcoholic could. It also indicated that strenuous work, one alcoholic with another, was vital to permanent recovery (Foreword to *Alcoholics Anonymous*, 2nd edition, 1955).

Later in AA's *Grapevine* magazine, however, Bill W. (1963) insisted that AA began in Zürich three years earlier than 'the Akron meeting' during a consultation between Carl Jung and an American alcoholic patient called Roland H. But since AA members believe that it is the mutual relationship of one problem drinker helping another that is the basis of Alcoholics Anonymous, they select the 1935 Akron meeting as being of particular significance in the official history of the movement.

A slightly different gloss was put on those early days in Henrietta Seiberling's (1971) message to the Akron AA group's Founders' Day meeting shortly after Bill Wilson's death. In contrast to the official history, she put much greater emphasis on the part played by members of the Akron Oxford group:

I would like to tell about Bob in the beginning. Bob and Ann came into the Oxford group . . . Someone spoke to me about Bob Smith's drinking. He didn't think that people knew it. And I decided that the people who shared in the Oxford group had never shared very costly things to make Bob lose his pride and share what he thought would cost him a great deal. So I decided to gather together some Oxford group people for a meeting . . . I warned Ann that I was going to have this meeting. I didn't tell her that it was for Bob, but I said, 'Come prepared to mean business. There is going to be no

pussyfooting around'. And we all shared very deeply our shortcomings, and what we had victory over. And then there was silence,
and I waited and thought, 'Will Bob say something?' Sure enough, in
that deep, serious tone of his, he says, 'Well, you good people have
all shared things that I am sure were very costly to you, and I am
going to tell you something which may cost me my profession. I am
a silent drinker, and I can't stop.' This was weeks before Bill came
to Akron.

From these accounts it appears that the move toward mutual support
in AA was not made because of some dissatisfaction with professional
helpers, but through the realisation that people with problems could help
each other and by doing so, help themselves. The next step for the
founders of AA, according to *Alcoholics Anonymous Comes of Age*,
was to go and work with other alcoholics, like Bill Dotson:

> 'Well, Bill', we said, 'can we come back and see you tomorrow?' 'Yes',
> he replied, 'you fellows really understand. Sure, I'd like to see you'.
> So the next day we came back and found him talking to his wife . . .
> Bill pointed to us and said, 'These are the fellows I was telling you
> about. They are the ones that know. They understand what this thing
> is all about.'
> Then Bill told us how, during the night, hope had dawned on him.
> If Bob and I could do it, he could do it. Maybe we could all do
> together what we could not do separately.

By August 1936, formal AA meetings had started. It had become
customary to set apart one night a week for a meeting, to be attended
by anyone and everyone who was interested. Apart from fellowship
and sociability, 'the prime object was to provide a time and place where
new people might bring their problems' (*Alcoholics Anonymous*, 1939).

In the forty years since those first Akron meetings, Alcoholics
Anonymous has grown into a world-wide organisation of groups. Trice
(1958) suggests that by 1944 the movement had 10,000 members in
300 groups in America and Canada and by 1957 had grown to 200,000
members and 7,000 groups throughout the world. In addition, there
were 1,000 seamen and 'lone' members in remote areas who maintained
contact with other AAs by mail. In its 1972 World Directory, Alcoholics
Anonymous gave details of 4,761 groups outside the U.S.A. and Canada
and although acknowledging that 'it is extremely difficult to obtain
completely accurate figures on AA's total membership at any given

time' felt able to say that '. . . as the result of a special census survey, total membership is estimated to be in excess of 575,000'. By 1974, the General Service Board were claiming that world membership had reached 800,000 and by 1977 well over 1,000,000.

In 1940, the trustees of the AA movement first published a mimeographed bulletin for the information of all members, which listed twenty-two cities in the United States in which groups were said to be 'well established and holding weekly meetings' (AA Bulletin 1940). In 1941 the trustees updated the list and included information, where it had been furnished, about the day of the week on which the groups met. In the year between the two lists the number of groups had grown from twenty-two to eighty-six. The 1941 list also noted that isolated AA members were in correspondence with the trustee-maintained World Service Office in New York from twenty-seven additional U.S. cities and three Canadian ones – Toronto, Vancouver and Montreal. This is the first record of AA activity outside the United States. There are groups now in well over a hundred different countries from Afghanistan to Zambia.

It is difficult to pinpoint exactly when the fellowship was established in Great Britain. During 1945 and 1946, a few individuals tried to achieve sobriety through correspondence with the Alcoholic Foundation in New York. Since there were so many American servicemen in England during the later stages of the war it is extremely unlikely that there were no *ad hoc* meetings of members. Nevertheless, the official history in the *AA Service Handbook for Great Britain* (1974) puts the earliest AA meeting as having taken place in the Dorchester Hotel, London, in March 1947.

In 1947, an American lady member who was visiting this country with her husband wrote to the five members who were in contact with the Foundation and arranged a meeting which took place in her room at the Dorchester Hotel, London, on 31 March 1947. A Canadian member whom she had met in a London restaurant on the previous Saturday and another lady member of the Hollywood Group whom she met on the boat coming over also attended. There were eight present at this meeting in the Dorchester, and it was probably the earliest AA meeting to take place in Great Britain.

From then on meetings were held in a variety of places: cinemas, cafés, restaurants and homes. After a time the members decided to advertise the existence of the Fellowship and a notice was produced which read, 'Alcoholism — a small body of anonymous ex-sufferers place themselves at the disposal of any requiring help; the offer is quite gratuitous'. Fifteen national newspapers either temporised or rejected the advertisement. One enquired how requests for help would be dealt with. The explanation resulted in a decision that the advertisement could be accepted. Only one newspaper, the *Financial Times*, finally agreed to run the advertisement, and the 'few' braced themselves for the expected deluge of letters. To their bitter disappointment there were only two letters, one post-marked 'Skegness' and the other 'North Wales'. However, meetings continued to take place more or less regularly in the homes of members and well wishers and in other places.

In autumn 1948, the first London group was formed. There were approximately a dozen members, but in January 1949 they produced the first monthly newsletter — twenty-five stencilled copies. This included a notice about an open meeting to be held the following month and concluded 'Let's stay sober. Just a reminder that we *are* alcoholics and that we should never be fooled by the thought that we can have just one for today'. The first provincial meeting was held in Manchester in December 1948. Scotland saw two meetings in 1950 and although Wales's first group met in Cardiff in 1957 and then disbanded, meetings took place in North Wales and began again in Cardiff in 1960. By 1959, the General Service Office in London was able to put out a list of over one hundred groups. Ten years later there were over five hundred and by 1978 there were well over one thousand.

The overall growth rate of Alcoholics Anonymous is very difficult to calculate. However, after the very rapid expansion of the first few years, recent computations have put the figure at between four and eight per cent during the 1960s and rising to fourteen per cent in 1973 (Seixas and Cadaret 1974). Chafetz and Demone (1962) argue that AA over-estimates its membership by twenty per cent as a result of over-lapping membership from group to group, particularly in cities. Bean's recent work (1975) suggests that membership increases to a certain per-centage in a particular area and then stops, and that increases in the overall size of Alcoholics Anonymous membership is accounted for by the geographical spread of groups. To date, there is no detailed study of how groups split or how new groups are established.

Closely allied to the question of membership is the question of 'success'; and adding to the difficulty of saying anything about either is the fact that, as a matter of policy, AA keeps no record of who goes to its meetings. This clearly undermines the possibility of making any systematic claim for the effectiveness of AA as compared with

other therapeutic or helping programmes (Bebbington 1976). Nevertheless, such claims *have* been made almost since its inception. In 1939, the
basic AA book, *Alcoholics Anonymous*, claimed that the organisation's
six year history had 'satisfactorily demonstrated that at least two out of
three alcoholics who wished to get well could apparently do so' while,
in an address to the American Psychiatric Association in 1943 Tiebout
relayed the following statistics from the New York office of AA:

5 recovered at the end of the first year
15 recovered at the end of the second year
40 recovered at the end of the third year
100 recovered at the end of the fourth year
400 recovered at the end of the fifth year
2000 recovered at the end of the sixth year
8000 recovered at the end of the seventh year

and said that 'Alcoholics Anonymous claims a recovery rate of seventy
five per cent of those who really try their methods' (Tiebout 1944).
Alcoholics Anonymous (1955) contains the following statement about
recovery which has often been quoted without qualification by other
writers:

Of alcoholics who came to AA, and really tried, 50% got sober at
once and remain that way; 25% sobered up after some relapses, and
among the remainder, those who stayed on with AA showed improvement. Other thousands came to a few AA meetings and at first
decided they did not want the program. But great numbers of them —
about two out of three — began to return as time passed.

Clearly, AA had no way of knowing this information. But clearly also,
given the fact that registers are not kept, it is difficult to make any kind
of precise estimate of the proportion of people who eventually 'get
sober' in AA.

This book is not primarily concerned with rates of success or with
comparisons between AA and other therapeutic regimes for people
whose drinking is causing them problems. The aim, rather, is to present
a description of the process by which members come together to help
each other to help themselves with their drink problems. Much too
much effort is wasted in the attempt to find out precisely how many
people are helped by some particular therapy or facility without first
looking at *how* they are helped.

Without being precise, it is clear that a large number of people have been helped in some way by Alcoholics Anonymous. This fact of contemporary life is not undermined by saying that such people might have been helped equally successfully by some other agency or that a proportion of them may well have got better spontaneously. The important point is that they and their intimates claim that their membership of AA was the one thing which made all the difference to the handling of their alcoholism. As such, we need to know much more about the mutual self-help process of Alcoholics Anonymous.

Organisation and Finance

We are not an organisation in the conventional sense of the word. Foreword to the first edition of *Alcoholics Anonymous* 1939

Alcoholics Anonymous is not organised in the formal or political sense. There are no governing officers, no rules or regulations, no fees or dues. *AA Fact File*, 1965

Alcoholics Anonymous is very keen to stress that it is not a real organisation, or not an organisation in the usual sense of the word. What they mean by that is that the basic philosophy of the way in which the fellowship operates is the reverse of the stereotypical industrial organisation.

Two central tenets of classical organisation theory are that there should be a division of labour and that this should be balanced by a unity of control. Adam Smith's description of the manufacturing of pins in his *Wealth of Nations*, published in 1776, is a classic illustration of the significance of division of labour. He noted that a worker by himself might produce twenty pins a day. But by breaking down the task of making pins into its many component operations – he estimated that there were about eighteen different jobs such as straightening the wire and cutting it – ten workers were able to produce 48,000 pins a day. This represented 4,800 pins per worker or 240 times what he could produce alone. The importance of unity of control, say the classic theorists, lies in the fact that the several different tasks have to be broken up into components by a central authority in line with a central plan of action; the efforts to each work unit need to be supervised, and the various jobs leading to the final product have to be co-ordinated.

Organisations, then, are taken to be instruments that enable certain goals to be realised. In order to attain such goals, organisations have a formally defined structure laid down in written rules and regulations.

In addition there is a hierarchy of control and a division of labour in which each member has a prescribed task. Etzioni's (1964) definition of an organisation reveals the core assumptions of such an approach.

> Organisations are social units (or human groupings) deliberately constructed and reconstructed to seek specific goals. . . Organisations are characterised by (1) divisions of labour, power and communications responsibilities, divisions which are not random or traditionally patterned, but deliberately planned to enhance the realisation of specific goals; (2) the presence of one or more power centres which control the concerted effort of the organisation and direct them toward its goals; these power centres also must review continuously the organisation's performance and repattern its structure, where necessary, to increase its efficiency; (3) substitution of personnel i.e. unsatisfactory persons can be removed and others assigned their task. The organisation can also recombine its personnel through transfer and promotion.

Alcoholics Anonymous, given that it is comprised of thousands of groups throughout the world, is 'organised'. But the nature of the organisation is the reverse of that outlined by Etzioni. Unlike the stereotypical business organisation the power lies at the periphery rather than the centre. The structure is determined by the mass of members not by the central committees, and the activities, practices and procedures of the organisation are all dependent upon the approval of the membership rather than being initiated by 'managers' at head office. The distinction between AA and a commercial organisation is highlighted by the title of the central committee. It is not a board of directors, or a board of management or a board of governors, each of which indicate where the focus of power is and in which way the authority flows. In AA the central committee is the General *Service* Board. The Bylaws of the General Service Board in America were adopted in 1957 and begin with the following words: 'The General Service Board of Alcoholics Anonymous Inc. now has but one purpose, that of serving the Fellowship of Alcoholics Anonymous' (*AA Service Manual* 1969). In Great Britain the General Service Board 'is the principal service vehicle of Conference, from whom it derives its authority in all service matters and to whom it gives an account of its stewardship in its Annual Report of Conference' (*The AA Service Handbook for Great Britain*, 1974).

The American Board consists of six non-alcoholic as well as thirteen

alcoholic members. In the early days non-alcoholic members out-
numbered the alcoholics. John Norris (1976), one of the non-alcoholic
members of the American Board explains why.

> It's interesting that when the board . . . first formed, nobody had
> had more than three years of sobriety in AA, and they didn't trust
> themselves, and didn't trust each other, in the money department. So
> the initial board was made up of a majority of non-alcoholics. There
> were eight non-alcoholics and seven alcoholics, up until 1962.

During its first decade, AA as a fellowship accumulated substantial
experience which indicated that certain group attitudes and principles
were particularly valuable in assuring survival of the informal structure
of the movement. In 1946, in their international journal *The AA
Grapevine,* these principles were reduced to writing by the founders
and early members as the 'Twelve Traditions of Alcoholics Anonymous'.
They were accepted and endorsed by the movement as a whole at the
first International Convention of AA at Cleveland, Ohio, in 1950.

1. Our common welfare should come first; personal recovery depends
upon AA unity.
2. For our group purpose there is but one ultimate authority — a
loving God as He may express Himself in our group conscience. Our
leaders are but trusted servants; they do not govern.
3. The only requirement for AA membership is a desire to stop
drinking.
4. Each group should be autonomous except in matters affecting
other groups or AA as a whole.
5. Each group has but one primary purpose — to carry its message to
the alcoholic who still suffers.
6. An AA group ought never endorse, finance or lend the AA name
to any related facility or outside enterprise lest problems of money,
property and prestige divert us from our primary purpose.
7. Every AA group ought to be fully self-supporting, declining
outside contributions.
8. Alcoholics Anonymous should remain forever non-professional,
but our service centers may employ special workers.
9. AA, as such, ought never be organized; but we may create service
boards or committees directly responsible to those they serve.
10. Alcoholics Anonymous has no opinion on outside issues; hence
the AA name ought never be drawn into public controversy.

11. Our public relations policy is based on attraction rather than promotion; we need always maintain personal anonymity at the level of press, radio and films.

12. Anonymity is the spiritual foundation of our traditions, ever reminding us to place principles before personalities.

Tradition 2 emphasises the basic principle that the members are the holders of authority for all AA services whether for groups, inter-groups, or for the fellowship as a whole.

The General Service Conference is the practical means by which group consciousness can express itself. The Conference is the key decision-making body for matters affecting the whole of the fellowship. Local groups send representatives to intergroups, which are groups of approximately fifteen local groups, which in turn elect delegates to the Annual Conference. Local groups, therefore, hold the key to who makes the decisions about the fellowship as a whole. There is no possibility of self-perpetuating cliques since no delegate can serve for more than three years after which they are ineligible for a further term as a delegate or appointed alternative delegate, either for the intergroup which elected them or for any other intergroup. Delegates from groups always outnumber members of the General Service Board by three or four to one. Alcoholic members of the General Service Board are elected for a term of six years, upon expiry of which they cease to be members and are not eligible for re-election at any future time. There is no fixed term for non-alcoholic members of the Board who serve as long as they are willing and able. Non-alcoholic members are asked to serve on the board when a vacancy occurs if they are felt to have something to contribute. The 1976 Annual Report of AA in Great Britain carried the following notice: The Board are pleased to report that Mr Jack Scrimgeour, Director of the Scottish Prison Service, accepted its invitation to be a non-alcoholic member and feel that his special experience will make an important contribution to the Fellowship.

All the talk of Conference and Boards should not deflect attention from the fact that AA's central office in London, with its secretary and volunteer support, is extremely small for an 'organisation' which has over a thousand basic units. The reason is, of course, that individual groups are autonomous and can quite easily function without any reference to central office, the board, conference or even an intergroup. All that is required for a group to come into existence is 'two or more alcoholics meeting together for purposes of sobriety'. They may then consider themselves an AA group 'providing that, as a group they are self-supporting and have no outside affiliation' (*World Directory* 1972b).

Over the years Alcoholics Anonymous has affirmed and strengthened a tradition of being fully self-supporting and not seeking or accepting contributions from non-members. When outside contributions are received at the General Service Office they are returned with a note explaining AA's position on the question of self-support. Individual contributions of as much as £5,000 have been declined in this way.

Expenses at the group level for the rental of meeting rooms, coffee, refreshments and literature are met by passing the hat at the end of each meeting. Groups are encouraged, but decide whether or not, to contribute a proportion of their collection to help with the running costs of the General Service Office. All member contributions are voluntary and there is a ceiling put on the amount which any individual can contribute in any one year.

Figures from the General Service Board in London (*Annual Report*, 1977) show that AA in England and Wales is expanding rapidly. Table 1.1 shows that between 1974 and 1976 the number of groups increased by almost forty per cent while the nett assets of Alcoholics Anonymous (Great Britain and Ireland) Ltd more than doubled.

Table 1.1: Recent Growth in Alcoholics Anonymous

	Groups in England and Wales		AA in G.B. and Ireland	
	Number	% increase	Nett Assets	% increase
1974	451		£23,511	
1975	534	18.4	£33,634	43.1
1976	619	15.9	£51,146	52.1

Although nett assets are increasing rapidly, the annual reports of the General Service Board reveal that members' direct contributions do not cover service expenditure. So in order for AA to balance its books, maintain its tradition of refusing all outside financing and avoid any need to have fixed dues or fees, it needs to make a profit from the *Share* journal, and from its books and pamphlets. Buying AA literature is the only way in which non-members can legitimately contribute to the fellowship's finances.

Table 1.2 shows that profits from literature sales have been increasing, but not as rapidly as the overall surplus of income over expenditure. Nevertheless, it is unusual for AA's profits from literature sales to be smaller than the overall surplus.

Table 1.2: Overall Surplus and Profit on Literature Sales

| | Income and Expenditure | | *Share*, Books and Pamphlets | |
	Overall Surplus	% increase	Profit	% increase
1974	£3,016		£7,696	
1975	£8,756	190.3	£11,897	54.6
1976	£16,133	84.3	£15,954	34.1

Members

The only requirement for AA membership is a desire to stop drinking.
Third Tradition of Alcoholics Anonymous

As was noted earlier, in the discussion of the question of success, there
has never been a competent long term study of who goes to Alcoholics
Anonymous. Several studies have looked at certain characteristics of AA
members in clinic populations, while several studies have looked at AA
volunteers and so probably evaluate the most successful members. AA
in the United States has conducted a national survey of itself in 1968,
1971, 1974 and 1977, while AA in Great Britain conducted a brief
survey in 1972. These studies, however, like the study which we
carried out, only report on a cross section of members at one point in
time. They only deal with people who happen to be attending meetings
during the study period.

A great deal of concern has been expressed lately by government
departments, professionals, and members of the general public, over
the growing number of women and young people who are developing
alcohol-related problems. Women and teenagers are accounting for an
increasing proportion of referrals to alcoholism clinics, convictions for
drunkenness offences and for road accidents in which alcohol appears to
have been a contributory factor. Alcoholics Anonymous claim to be
attracting more women and young people to the fellowship. Their
booklet, *44 Questions and Answers about the AA Program of
Recovery from Alcoholism* (1952a), says that 'the number of women
who are finding help in AA for their drinking problem increases daily'
and that 'one of the most heartening trends in the growth of AA is the
fact that more and more young men and women are attracted to the
programme *before* their problem drinking results in complete disaster'.

Our survey of Alcoholics Anonymous members, taken in conjunction with two previous British surveys conducted in 1964 (Edwards *et al.* 1967) and 1972 (AA 1972a), presents an opportunity to see whether changes in the structure of the alcoholic population are reflected in AA membership. It is clear from Table 1.3 that the proportion of women members of Alcoholics Anonymous in England and Wales has increased substantially since 1964. On the other hand, there is no evidence that the growing number of young people with severe alcohol-related problems is reflected in the fellowship. The average age of AA members was no lower in 1976 than it was in 1964.

Table 1.3: Sex Ratio and Age of AA Members in 1964, 1972 and 1976

Date	Men : Women	Average Age
1964	4.2 : 1	45.7
1972	3.5 : 1	47.3
1976	1.7 : 1	46.4

It could be argued that an increasing number of young people *are* joining AA but that this fact is masked, in the average age figures, by members staying longer in the fellowship. Table 1.4, however, gives no support to this idea. It shows that, for both men and women, the age at which current members joined Alcoholics Anonymous has remained remarkably constant for the past dozen years.

Table 1.4: Current AA Members, Sex and Age on Joining

Year of Joining	Men Age on Joining	Women Age on Joining	Total Age on Joining
1976	44.8	37.2	41.9
1975–72	44.8	39.0	42.2
1971–68	40.9	38.0	40.2
1967–64	38.2	40.4	38.8
1963–	40.2	39.4	40.1

In relation to any organisation which grows as rapidly as Alcoholics Anonymous has done, the question arises of whether the expanded membership is 'the same as' the original. As we have already seen, the proportion of women members has changed. But in an organisation which deals with problems it is important to try and find out whether the large number of new members have the same kind of problems as members in previous years. Is there any evidence, for example, that the new members have gone to AA earlier in the course of their alcoholism, having suffered fewer problems, or before they reached 'rock bottom'? The AA booklet, *44 Questions* (1952a), says that in the early days of the movement 'it was commonly thought that the only logical candidates for AA were those men and women who had lost their jobs, had hit Skid Row, had completely disrupted their family life or had otherwise isolated themselves from normal social relationships over a period of years'. This 'out-of-date picture' of AA members is contrasted with the new younger membership, the majority of whom 'still have jobs and families. Many have never been jailed or committed to institutions. But they . . . recognise that they are alcoholics and they see no point in letting alcoholism run its inevitable disastrous course'.

The present survey asked members to say whether they had suffered any of a series of physical, mental and social problems associated with alcohol consumption. Since some of these problems, particularly the physical and social ones, were similar to those which Edwards (1967) asked about in his 1964 survey of AA members, it was possible to see whether current members reported fewer problems, or 'complications' as Edwards called them, than members twelve years previously.

We have already questioned AA's claim that its membership is getting younger. Table 1.5 shows that there is little evidence, either, that people are now joining the fellowship with fewer problems.

In seven out of the fourteen comparisons, the 1976 figure is within five per cent plus or minus the 1964 figure. In two cases the 1964 figure is more than five per cent lower than the 1976 figure and in five cases it is more than five per cent higher. It is clear, from Table 1.5, that men and women members admit to a very similar amount of physical, mental and family problems. But, as in 1964, more women than men have tried to commit suicide, while more men than women have lost a job, been in fights, had trouble with the police and had severe financial problems.

So while AA is expanding rapidly and has responded to the growing number of women alcoholics, it appears to have completely failed to attract any significant proportion of the growing number of young people for whom drink is causing problems. Judging by members' reports of their physical, mental and social problems, AA does not appear, either, to be picking up people any earlier in the process of their alcoholism. This suggests that Alcoholics Anonymous is still, for most people, a last hope organisation.

Table 1.5: Members' Alcohol-related Problems 1976 and 1964

	Men		Women		Total	
Problems	1976 %	(1964) (%)	1976 %	(1964) (%)	1976 N	%
Physical						
Blackouts	88.9	(95.0)	83.9	(91.0)	149	87.1
Too drunk to stand	85.2		87.1		147	85.9
Severe morning shakes	79.6	(84.0)	76.2	(72.0)	131	77.1
'Seeing things'	44.4		41.9		75	43.5
DTs	38.0		37.1		65	35.3
'Heard voices'	38.9	(48.0)	29.0	(38.0)	61	33.6
Mental						
Deep shame	89.8		96.8		158	92.4
Extremely depressed	90.7		91.9		156	91.2
Extremely frightened	82.4		83.9		141	82.9
Uncontrollable anger	67.6		67.7		115	67.6
Unable to trust anyone	62.0		59.7		104	61.2
Attempted suicide	34.3	(26.0)	48.4	(47.0)	68	39.4
Social						
Neglected the family	72.8		70.5		124	71.7
Severe money problems	66.7		37.7		98	56.0
Trouble with police	62.9		26.2		87	49.4
Lost a job	58.1	(63.0)	31.1	(43.0)	85	48.2
Broken marriage	38.1	(35.0)	44.3	(28.0)	72	40.4
Been in fights	38.1	(40.0)	21.3	(19.0)	58	31.9

The Programme of Recovery

The relative success of the AA program seems to be due to the fact that an alcoholic who no longer drinks has an exceptional facility for reaching and helping an uncontrolled drinker. *AA Fact File* 1965

The local group meeting is the centre and heart of the AA recovery programme since, as Leach and associates (1969) have pointed out, the meeting is usually 'the first and only distinguishable AA activity in which all the members of a local group participate at the same time'. Indeed, it is a familiar part of AA practice to recommend that newcomers go to 'ninety meetings in ninety days'. For the newcomer these would be 'open' rather than 'closed' meetings.

An open meeting of AA is a group meeting that any member of the community, alcoholic or non-alcoholic, may attend. The only obligation is that of not disclosing the names of AA members outside the meeting. A typical open meeting will have a chairperson who opens and closes the meeting and introduces other speakers. With rare exceptions, the speakers at an open meeting are AA members. Each, in turn, may review some of his drinking experiences which led to his joining AA. Or he may give his interpretation of the recovery programme and suggest what his sobriety has meant to him. Most open meetings conclude with a social period during which coffee and refreshments are served and members can talk informally with each other and any newcomers who are present.

A closed meeting is limited to members of the local AA group, or to visiting members from other groups. The purpose of closed meetings is to give members an opportunity to discuss particular phases of their alcoholic problems which they feel can be understood best only by other alcoholics.

Given that all members are alcoholic it may be surprising to outsiders to find that the one topic which is almost never discussed is 'What is alcoholism?' The basic assumption in Alcoholics Anonymous concerning alcoholism is that it is not a moral weakness but a disease, sometimes called an allergy. AA philosophy encourages its members, and the general public, to believe that alcoholism is a disease which, once contracted, can never be cured. The most that can be hoped for is that the condition is arrested. This is what AA members mean when they say 'once an alcoholic always an alcoholic' and then talk about recovering from alcoholism. Recovery means recognising that, for some reason, the AA member is suffering from this disease, that it can never be cured, that, therefore, alcohol can play no part in the member's life, and that recovery depends on maintaining sobriety, the one goal of the Alcoholics Anonymous programme. As the AA preamble puts it, 'our primary purpose is to stay sober and help other alcoholics to achieve sobriety'.

Recovery from the disease of alcoholism is the focus of the AA programme rather than the search for causes of the condition, and recovery is a complex process with the opportunity for people to find sobriety in any one of a variety of different ways. Nevertheless, there are certain guiding principles which were developed by the early members which have remained more or less unchanged. These principles are printed in every meeting list and in most of the special pamphlets produced by AA and are elaborated in detail in *Twelve Steps and Twelve Traditions* (1952b). The heart of the AA programme of personal recovery is contained in the 'twelve suggested steps' which describe the experiences of the early members.

THE TWELVE STEPS

1. We admitted we were powerless over alcohol — that our lives had become unmanageable.
2. Came to believe that a Power greater than ourselves could restore us to sanity.
3. Made a decision to turn our will and our lives over to the care of God *as we understood Him*.
4. Made a searching and fearless moral inventory of ourselves.
5. Admitted to God, to ourselves and to another human being the exact nature of our wrongs.
6. Were entirely ready to have God remove all these defects of character.
7. Humbly asked Him to remove our shortcomings.
8. Made a list of all persons we had harmed, and became willing to make amends to them all.
9. Made direct amends to such people wherever possible, except when to do so would injure them or others.
10. Continued to take personal inventory and when we were wrong, promptly admitted it.
11. Sought through prayer and meditation to improve our conscious contact with God *as we understood Him*, praying only for knowledge of His will for us and the power to carry that out.
12. Having had a spiritual awakening as the result of these steps, we tried to carry this message to alcoholics and to practice these principles in all our affairs.

While these steps embody many core principles of the AA programme the newcomer is not expected to accept or follow them 'in their entirety if he feels unwilling or unable to do so' (*AA Fact File*, 1965). The steps themselves clearly stress faith, abdication of personal responsibility, passivity in the hands of God, confession of wrong doing and, finally, response to spiritual awakening by sharing it with others.

From the outset Alcoholics Anonymous has been described as a religious movement which is hardly surprising since, as Edwards (1964) points out 'a feature of the twelve steps . . . is that alcohol and alcoholism are each mentioned once while God is mentioned five times'. There has been serious theological debate about the compatibility of the twelve steps with the teaching of the Catholic Church, while AA has been described as a socio-religious group in which the primary goal is 'the "good life" here and now' (Ritchie 1948). Mowrer (1961) sees AA as 'the emerging church of the twenty-first century' and Gellman (1964) as 'a formal organisation of a group of worshippers who share a common and defined set of beliefs and rituals concerning sacrificed objects and entities they revere'. Jones (1970) has drawn out several parallels between Alcoholics Anonymous and sectarian movements and found that eighty-eight per cent of a sample of AA members admitted to a 'conversion'.

By contrast to these outside commentators, Alcoholics Anonymous claims to be 'spiritual' rather than religious and that the 'power greater than ourselves' can mean any power. Their position is succinctly set out in *44 Questions and Answers about the AA Program of Recovery from Alcoholism* (1952a) in answer to the question, Is AA a Religious Society?

> AA is not a religious society, it requires no definite religious belief as a condition of membership. Although it has been endorsed and approved by many religious leaders, it is not allied with any organisation or sect. Included in its membership are Catholics, Protestants, Jews and even a sprinkling of those who still consider themselves atheists or agnostics.
>
> The AA programme of recovery from alcoholism is undeniably based on acceptance of certain spiritual values. The individual member is free to interpret those values as he thinks best, or not to think about them at all, if he so elects.
>
> Before he turned to AA, the average alcoholic had already admitted that he could not control his drinking. Alcohol had, for him, become a power greater than himself, and it had been accepted in those terms. AA suggests that, to achieve and maintain sobriety, the alcoholic needs to accept and depend upon another Power that he recognizes is greater than himself. Some alcoholics choose to consider the AA group itself as the Power greater than

themselves, while others choose to accept still different concepts of this Power. But most AAs adopt the concept of God, as *He may be understood by the individual himself.*

Some members, for example, found their 'power' in other members or, like Eddie (1975), in the group.

> When I got sober some time ago, my faith in God had long since gone.
> Any mention of the word God got me good and mad, but step two
> says 'Came to believe that a power greater than ourselves could
> restore us to sanity'. Now a lot of AAs assume this power to be
> something divine. The power as I see it, is the combined power of
> all the thousands of alcoholics in AA who are, let's face it, anything
> but divine.

Others, like Andrew, make the point even more forcefully;

> I said, 'It's nothing to do with God! . . . If you want to believe in
> God, then that's your pigeon.' So I picked on a piece of wire on
> the floor and I said, 'That could be your God'. There was a guy in
> here who was an Irishman. He hated Englishmen. He went to an AA
> meeting and they told him, 'Do what you like. If hating Englishmen
> keeps you sober, then hate them'.

Bean (1975) suggests that it might be helpful to see that the Twelve Steps actually represent a complex internal process that involves a semi-religious conversion — despair, seeing the light, hope, changed behaviour — a mechanism for assuaging guilt — confession, penance — and an emotional shift from isolated helplessness and dependency that includes a capacity to take responsibility for controlling drinking. In psychotherapeutic terms, she says, the steps include:
1. Breakdown of denial concerning alcoholism, or at least some beginning on this direction.
2. Reassurance and instillation of hope, permitting abandonment of denial.
3. Shift of responsibility away from oneself through assumption of a dependency stance toward an authority figure.
4–7. Confession and catharsis.
8, 9. Making amends — penance and undoing.
10. A mechanism to continue catharsis and undoing.
11. Continuing confirmation of a new image of oneself.

12. Through helping others and recruiting new members, redirection of energy through altruism and sublimation.

Several writers have seen Alcoholics Anonymous as a social movement. Toch (1965), for example, says it is the kind of social movement which produces changes within its members rather than in society, but in which:

> Each individual's efforts to solve his own problems become part of his efforts to solve a social problem — one with which he is intimately familiar, and about which he has reasons to be concerned. Since the member has learned to see himself as an example of a general problem, he can view his efforts as directed at both the particular and universal goal.

Apart from seeing Alcoholics Anonymous as a religious or as a social movement there is a whole range of other interpretations of the AA programme. Some see Alcoholics Anonymous working because it relieves stress, tension and anxiety (e.g. Maxwell 1962), others because it supplies a control for emotional immaturity and gives the responsibility to make members emotionally mature (e.g. Chambers 1953); or is a mother substitute providing affection and satisfying personality needs such as centredness (e.g. Bonacker 1958); or provides religion which is inherent to man (e.g. Tiebout 1961); or fills an existential meaning vacuum (e.g. Holmes 1970); or provides necessary intimate primary group relations which overcome isolation (e.g. Bales 1945); or provides self-reliant, adaptive competence at problem solving (e.g. Killilea 1976). Other commentators, rather than presupposing some fundamental lack on the part of the member, see AA 'working' as a result of setting certain goals which reinforce abstention (e.g. Clancy 1964) or which promote 'object choice' and 'object love' (e.g. Stewart 1955), or by destigmatising and relabelling which reconstructs the member's existence by resocialising him into a new subculture (e.g. Bacon 1957).

This view of AA as a sub-culture or 'way of life' is widely held. Both members themselves and outsiders feel that the fellowship's closely knit values constitute a sub-culture which fundamentally differentiates AA from the kind of therapy offered by psychiatric or other helping organisations. AA themselves (*44 Questions and Answers*, 1952a) see the fellowship as providing a new way of life for those who follow its programme closely.

A NEW WAY OF LIFE

A way of life cannot truly be described; it must be lived. Descriptive literature that relies upon broad, inspirational generalities is bound to leave many questions unanswered and many readers not fully satisfied that they have come upon the thing they need and seek. At the other extreme, a catalogue of the mechanics and details of a programme for living can portray only part of the value of such a programme.

AA is a programme for a new way of life without alcohol, a programme that is working successfully for hundreds of thousands of men and women who approach it and apply it with honesty and sincerity. It is working throughout the world and for men and women in all stations and walks of life.

The most important aspect of AA for Gellman (1964) 'is the socialisation process which leads to AA as "a way of life" '. In effect, he says 'a subculture is created in which the status of alcoholic has positive connotations'. This idea of transforming a stigmatised feature or characteristic into something positive is one of the themes which run through the growing amount of literature which places Alcoholics Anonymous within the broader context of mutual support or self-help groups (Robinson and Henry 1977). Indeed AA is often taken to be the archetypal self-help group. As such it is seen as resolving the alcoholic crisis by allaying the symptom and handling the social stigma; by giving information and guidance on the problem; and by providing a supporting community (Killilea 1976). For Kropotkin (1944), the support obtained through mutual aid is essential to survival, with ties of mutual aid 'playing a significant part in maintaining psychological and physical integrity of the individual over time' (Caplan 1974).

Clearly, the range of interpretations of Alcoholics Anonymous is immense. And, as Bean (1975) says, explanations of the AA process often tend to do little more than reveal the interpretive schema of the particular disciplines within which the interpreters operate.

Sociologists tend to describe AA as a psycho-social re-educating tool or a chance for relabelling; anthropologists as a process of acculturation; theologians as a framework for spiritual conversion and change; and psychiatrists and other mental health workers as a form of therapy.

The emphasis of this book will be to place Alcoholics Anonymous firmly within the context of mutual aid and self-help.

2 BECOMING A MEMBER

> Numerous alcoholics have responded to Alcoholics Anonymous
> upon first exposure, often without subsequent 'slips'. Still
> others react neutrally, or even antagonistically, and remain
> unattracted to the group and its program for sobriety. (Trice
> 1959)

Anyone familiar with the world of alcoholism will find it easy to think
of people who, for no obvious reason, managed to 'get on' in AA right
from their first contact with the fellowship, and to think of others who,
again for no obvious reason, found the programme totally unacceptable.
This question of who affiliates and who does not has puzzled many
people. They are unable to accept AA's explanation, that some people
are 'ready' for AA while others are not, since this merely pushes the
matter one stage further back to the question of what constitutes
readiness.

In much of the early literature on AA there is an awareness of the
problem of non-affiliation and several 'hunches as to its explanation'
(Trice 1957). Bill W. (1949), one of the two co-founders of AA, felt that
non-affiliates had 'powerful rationalisation to be broken down'. Wilson
(1951) was baffled by the inability of some to join: 'With all the
advantages AA offers, one cannot resist speculating on what
characterises these potential recruits who are unable to profit from
membership'. However, she offers no speculations. Affiliated
alcoholics are often described as being more receptive to AA principles.
Jellinek (1946), for example, speaks of some alcoholics as 'being those
types who are attracted to AA', but does not indicate what constitutes
these 'types'. Ritchie (1948) asks the question, 'How does the factor
of selectivity operate with reference to the types and classes of people
who become AAs?' but suggests no answer.

Still others mention personality factors. Brown (1950), after
dividing a sample of alcoholics into neurotics and psychopaths, by the
Minnesota Multiphasic Personality Inventory, concluded that 'the
neurotic drinker may be more likely to respond to the supportive
group measures offered by AA'. Chambers (1953) states that 'most of
those who become members have been lonely, isolated people who in
the course of their abnormal drinking lives have lost their friends and
contact with society', while Jackson and Conner (1953) suggest that

'AA may be more successful with the Skid Row alcoholic because it manipulates the pattern of group behavior which he already possesses toward a new end, sobriety'.

In the light of what he termed this 'meagre' literature on affiliation, Trice (1957, 1959) conducted a number of studies in an attempt to compare the experiences and attitudes of affiliates and non-affiliates during three phases of the affiliation process: before going to any meetings at all, at the time of the initial contact with a group and after attending meetings for a few weeks. In two areas, particularly, Trice found sharp differentiation between the two groups. The affiliates, in contrast to the non-affiliates, regarded themselves before they ever attended a meeting, as people 'who often shared their troubles with others'. Furthermore, after attending meetings for a few weeks, the affiliates, in much greater numbers than the non-affiliates, were attracted to the casual, informal interactions that occurred before and after the formal AA meeting. These two findings suggested to Trice that a stronger emotional need for social acceptance existed among affiliates than among non-affiliates, 'apparently an "affiliation motive" was aiding those who successfully joined AA, but was relatively weak in those who did not'.

Rather than attempting to identify other features which distinguish the affiliate from the non-affiliates, this chapter concentrates on the question of *how* people affiliate and become members of Alcoholics Anonymous.

Whether or not a person who has some problem decides that some particular self-help group is for him depends on the way he sees the problem and the image he has of what the group is and what it is for. There is a range of situations in which people may see self-help groups as inappropriate for them. Clearly people who do not think that they have a problem, or see their difficulty as a normal part of everyday living, are unlikely to be interested in self-help or any other form of help. Those who do not drink, or if they do drink see no problem in it, are unlikely to be interested in contacting an AA group. As the General Secretary of AA put it, 'nobody comes through an AA door for kicks. You don't go for fun. Why bother going to an AA meeting if you have no problems?'

The point is, however, that a person can have a great many problems, but not see that drink is causing them or related to them in any way. Someone may enjoy some or even all aspects of drinking. These activities *can* be associated with 'problems' such as being drunk, in debt or in court. But if this person sees AA as concerned only with drinking while he sees his problem as 'having worries' or 'being unlucky' or 'being picked on' then he is unlikely to consider AA as in any way relevant to his situation. The story of Peter's drinking problem illustrates how both the drinker and professional helpers can fail to recognise what later is seen as the development of a severe drinking problem.

Peter's Drinking Problem

Peter was sixteen when he left school and he had never had a drink in his life. His father drank heavily but his mother not at all. Apart from English and Music, Peter was bad at most things. Not only that, but he was very unhappy as well.

> I was very shy and I was absolutely hopeless at lessons. I hated school. I detested it. I got bullied and all the usual things and just couldn't wait to leave. When I did leave school and got away from my father and when I got a job I thought everything would be lovely. But, of course, it wasn't.

From his first day as an office junior he realised that leaving school had solved nothing. He was still desperately unhappy. He was still a loner. On his own he would often just walk around in the dark with his only 'friend' a portable radio. Life was a deadly routine: up in the morning, no breakfast, rush to the tube, boring tasks all day at work, and then back to the bedsitter where he 'avoided the landlady and spent the evenings imagining that everyone else in London was having the time of their lives'. He was bitter, but no one knew. And if they had done, 'who would have cared?' This was Peter's life for almost two years. 'Then I discovered drink!'

Several people from the office used to call into the local pub on their way home. They would often talk about it the next day and seemed, to Peter, to have been having 'a really great time'. They had given up asking Peter to go with them because he always refused, until:

> This Friday when Gerry, the lad who did the post, was leaving to go into the Army. Everybody went round to the Bush and, because Gerry really got at me, I went along as well. I can't remember what I actually had first, but I certainly had cider that evening. I've heard people say that they've ended up on cider, well, I started on it. It was really strong stuff from a china jar. Well, that was my drink from then on, oh, for months. It was like a duck to water, and I

almost had enough to swim in sometimes'.

From being a permanent outsider, Peter became, almost overnight, one of the regulars. With the cider he felt he was able to mix with people. But it was not without problems. 'Hangovers were part of every-day life as well. I used to get some pretty vile heads, even in the early days. I went on to gin and cider mixed. Formula One it was called'.

Peter's life had changed dramatically. He moved into a flat with three of his closest drinking friends and work became a part-time chore for raising funds to 'enjoy life'. He got sacked from one job for being absent and left several others because he got 'pushed around'. Money became a problem. 'I'd never got enough money to cope with the kind of life I wanted. So I kept in with people that had a bit more money than me'. Peter began to help out after hours in a pub where he was a regular. Then he decided to work in pubs fulltime, where the opportunities for drinking were almost limitless. But actually drink was not the main attraction at this stage. It was 'the atmosphere that attracted. The louder the music the better. I could be, not the main attraction, but I got plenty of attention being the barman as well'. Eventually Peter managed to get a job where he could live on the premises. 'Often I'd got the pub to myself. I could do the bars, drink as much as I wanted to. I'd got more in my bedroom than they'd got in the bar, I think. My wardrobe was loaded with the stuff'. And, of course, he was drinking in the mornings, as soon as he woke up, 'because of the nerves'.

'Nerves' was Peter's word for a whole range of feelings of misery and depression. He tried to lift the depression by drinking even more. In the end, though, he went to his doctor who, after a 'two-minute' consul-tation, gave him a prescription for Valium. Drink was never mentioned by either of them. The Valium was 'marvellous' for a while. But Peter soon went over the dose, and took more and more. A bottle would only last a few days, and then he would be back for more, 'when the booze didn't work it was the pills and when the pills didn't work it was the booze, and then both of them together'. Even after all this neither he nor his doctor thought that drink was a problem.

No, I never gave booze a second thought as being a problem. It was my nerves that were the thing, the shaking hands and headaches. I'd been having hot and cold sweats and nightmares. Perspiring and wetting the bed.

Eventually after three suicide attempts, many fights, and several dud cheques slipped into bar tills in exchange for cash, came the episode which changed everything.

> Well, I started serving and you know what it's like on Saturdays. People in with their wives and pretending they don't know you as well as they do. The regulars that is. Anyway I was in a violent mood. I hadn't eaten all day. Then I told them all to 'f- off', called them names and started throwing glasses. There were all these big mirrors at the back of the pub so I had a field day.

Peter then went out into the car park, cut his hand on a car wing mirror, and 'weeping and wailing' went down to the railway line where he was found by the police.

> They got the law out to protect me from myself. By this time I was on the lines. Oh yes, the old railway lines were useful. I used to wander up and down them and wait. But, of course, no trains ever came. By the time I used to get there, about midnight, there were no trains running.

The police took him off to hospital to have his hand stitched up. His arms were black and blue, his watch was smashed. 'Then they said to me, rather than charging me, had I thought of going to Fairlawnes, the mental hospital?' By now, seven years after leaving school, Peter was several hundred pounds in debt, his parents had refused to see him any more, a maintenance order was being processed and physically he was a wreck.

> So I went into hospital but it was for a nervous breakdown. It wasn't for booze even then. They kept me on the pills which was good. But booze wasn't mentioned. I saw the psychiatrist and he spoke about my emotional life and all that side, but never the booze.

However, after coming back to the ward drunk a few times from 'the pub at the bottom of the hill' Peter decided to discharge himself. He was very depressed. The charge nurse told him that if he did discharge himself, it might be very difficult to get back in again.

> Then he said, 'Have you ever thought of AA?' And I hadn't. I just

thought of the automobile people. I'd never given AA a thought.
Anyway two people just came along to see me and that was the
start of it. Thank God.

Making Contact with AA

Peter, clearly, had a great many problems and yet neither he nor his GP
nor the hospital psychiatrist saw his drinking as being of great importance. This is a familiar situation. Most people who go to self-help
groups are faced with a whole range of everyday problems of living and
part of the task of self-help groups is to help people to settle, from
among their many problems, on to one clearly defined set of problems
and acknowledge their centrality. Much of the publicity material put
out by self-help groups is designed to help potential members to do
just that. Simple questionnaires are often a key part of the publicity
package, which aim to help people to accept the *possibility* that they
might be 'overweight', 'a compulsive gambler', or 'a child batterer', or
'an alcoholic'. And, usually, anybody who does the thing which could
cause 'the problem' will find something in the questionnaire to worry
about. Almost anyone who, for example, gambles would be able to say
'yes' to the seven out of twenty questions that, according to Gamblers
Anonymous, would signify that they were a compulsive gambler.

Who me?, one of AA's small pamphlets asks, 'Are You An
Alcoholic?' and lists the following questions.

1. Do you lose time from work due to drinking?
2. Is drinking making your home life unhappy?
3. Do you drink because you are shy with other people?
4. Is drinking affecting your reputation?
5. Have you ever felt remorse after drinking?
6. Have you gotten into financial difficulties as a result of drinking?
7. Do you turn to lower companions and an inferior environment
    when drinking?
8. Does your drinking make you careless of your family's welfare?
9. Has your ambition decreased since drinking?
10. Do you crave a drink at a definite time daily?
11. Do you want a drink the next morning?
12. Does drinking cause you to have difficulty in sleeping?
13. Has your efficiency decreased since drinking?
14. Is drinking jeopardising your job or business?
15. Do you drink to escape from worries or trouble?
16. Do you drink alone?

17. Have you ever had a complete loss of memory as a result of drinking?
18. Has your physician ever treated you for drinking?
19. Do you drink to build up your self-confidence?
20. Have you ever been to a hospital or institution on account of drinking?

It is difficult to imagine that many drinkers would not be able to answer 'yes' to one of the twenty questions and so be worried that they 'may be an alcoholic'. AA say that 'if you have answered YES to any *two* the chances are that you *are an alcoholic*' while 'if you have answered "yes" to *three or more, you are definitely an alcoholic*'. The next page of the pamphlet begins 'Here's Hope For You', and gives a brief description of AA. It is not necessary for the person at this stage to believe that he *is* an alcoholic, but just to acknowledge the possibility. The real work of translating that possibility into a certainty begins when the drinker meets an AA member face-to-face. But in order to meet a member face-to-face a drinker has to know that AA exists and many people do not. Only a small proportion of the AA members in England and Wales knew anything about how AA worked before drink became a problem. As Table 2.1 shows, a quarter of them had never even heard of the fellowship.

Table 2.1: Knowledge of AA before Drink becomes a Problem

Knowledge of AA	Men %	Women %	Total N	%
Knew something about AA	10.2	12.9	19	11.2
Had only *heard* of AA	68.5	56.5	109	64.1
Had *never heard* of AA	21.3	30.6	42	24.7

Clearly, then, most people do not make a totally independent choice about whether or not to go to AA and, as Table 2.2 shows, members were able to identify a whole range of major influences on their decision to go to the first meeting. Family members, people who were already members of AA, and members of the medical profession were cited most often, with AA members being more influential for men and psychiatrists for women.

Table 2.2: People involved in the Decision to go to the First AA Meeting

People Involved	Men %	Women %	Total N	%
Family	47.2	51.6	82	48.8
An AA member	42.5	25.8	61	36.3
Psychiatrist	23.6	40.3	50	29.8
GP	18.9	17.7	31	18.5
Friends	9.4	16.1	20	11.9
Social Worker	6.6	9.7	13	7.7
Probation Officer	1.9	1.6	3	1.8
Employer	2.8	—	3	1.8

Being Twelfth Stepped

At some stage, either at the first meeting or sometimes before even going to a meeting, the drinker comes face-to-face with an AA member. This first real contact with AA is called twelfth stepping: after the last of the steps in the programme of recovery: 'Step twelve, having had a spiritual awakening as the result of the steps we tried to carry this message to alcoholics and practise these principles in all our affairs'. At this first meeting between the drinker and the AA member the new-comer's condition is not defined as alcoholism and he is not told that he is an alcoholic. As one long-standing member explained:

> You see the only qualification for membership is the desire to stop drinking. It's not that you have a label on you — 'I am an alcoholic' — it's a desire to stop drinking. Now AA doesn't tell you that you are an alcoholic. It can only help you arrive at your own personal decision. AA doesn't go out to get recruits for membership. We're not going into pubs, seeing somebody drunk and saying, 'Chum, you are an alcoholic come and join us'. But if you come to us, you're making the first move, then we can help and this is done by what we call twelfth stepping.

Much twelfth stepping, however, is not merely waiting for the drinker to make 'the first move'. Experienced members try to pick the right moment to begin the twelfth step process, often by working in league with the drinker's family, friends and doctor. The aim is to try and introduce the AA message at 'just the right moment' when the potential member appears most likely to be receptive to it. 'When you

discover a prospect for Alcoholics Anonymous', says 'the Big Book'
(*Alcoholics Anonymous*, 1939), 'find out all you can about him. If he
does not want to stop drinking, don't waste time trying to persuade
him. You may spoil a later opportunity'. Whenever possible the
twelfth step approach is made direct to the drinker and not through
the family. 'Though you have talked with the family, leave them out of
the first discussion. Under these conditions your prospect will see he
is under no pressure'. Then comes the vital meeting. Again, *Alcoholics
Anonymous* (1939) explains in detail the precise form that this first
contact should take:

> See your man alone if possible. At first engage in general conver-
> sation. After a while, turn the talk to some phase of drinking. Tell
> him enough of your drinking habits, symptoms and experiences. . .
> When he sees you know all about the drinking game, commence
> to describe yourself as an alcoholic . . . how you finally learned
> that you 'were sick'. Give him an account of the struggles that
> made you stop. . . Continue to speak of alcoholism as an illness,
> a fatal malady . . . keep his attention focussed mainly on your
> personal experience. . . Even though your protege may not have
> entirely admitted his condition, he has become curious to know
> how you got well. *Tell him exactly what happened to you . . .*
> outline the program of action, explain how you made a self-
> appraisal, how you straightened out your past and why you are
> now endeavoring to be helpful to him.

As the General Secretary of AA put it, 'one can only hope that
whatever they may be thinking, whatever doubts they may have, they
may be able to identify with you'. Identification is the core of the
twelfth step contact. The aim is to get the potential member to listen
to the experiences of the AA member and to see so much of himself in
the story that he 'realises' that if the AA member is 'an alcoholic' then
'I must be an alcoholic too'. This certainly works for some people.
As John said:

> Well, I just listened to him, this was the twelfth step call when I
> was in hospital and feeling pretty desperate, and he told me his
> drinking story. And I began to pick it up and think, 'Oh yes'. You
> can identify with different things that I may have done or felt. 'Oh,
> I've done them as well' you think, the similar ups and downs, all
> sorts of things, the mental side especially. It was as if he'd opened

up my little brain and was reading my lot.

It is a simple business after a reaction like this for the AA member to persuade the potential member to go to an AA meeting.

Not everyone, of course, responds to the twelfth step message in this way. Many alcoholics see the hand of their family and friends behind the visit, or they reject the efforts of hospitals to pressure them into seeing someone from AA. Among the patients attending the Maudsley out-patient alcoholism clinic were some who had been approached by an AA member and found the message unacceptable. In a series of fifty patients who were interviewed thirty-two had been to an AA meeting at some time or other. Of the other eighteen, nine had been in contact with someone from AA.

> I saw this bloke and he said he was an AA member and then he
> started telling me his tale. It was in a pub and I thought
> he seemed a bit of a holy Joe. I told him to piss off.

> I didn't like the way I was approached. I didn't like this person
> tabbing me wherever I went.

> It was embarrassing. He started telling me about all his past mis-
> demeanours and I didn't know him from Adam. I thought if that's
> what I'll be like they can keep it.

Not surprisingly, these people did not 'identify' and go happily along to the nearest AA meeting. They had very clear ideas about what AA was like and they wanted nothing to do with it.

Going to the First Meeting

The fact that, as we saw earlier, many people knew very little about AA before they became involved and were in many cases persuaded into going by their family or doctor makes it unsurprising to find, in Table 2.3, that over half of current members did not think that AA could help at all when they went to their first meeting.

Although so many of the current members were pressurised into going to meetings of an organisation which they did feel could help them, something obviously happened to encourage them to get involved since, as Table 2.4 shows, fifty per cent of them went to more than one meeting a week over the next four weeks.

There are no set rules for how many meetings a newcomer ought to

Table 2.3: Whether Members thought AA could Help

	Men %	Women %	Total N	Total %
Thought AA could help	20.4	18.2	30	19.6
Did not know	25.5	25.5	39	25.5
Did not think AA could help	54.1	56.4	84	54.9

Table 2.4: Number of Meetings attended in the First Four Weeks

Number of Meetings	Men %	Women %	Total N	Total %
1 − 4	47.6	54.1	83	50.0
5 − 8	20.0	13.1	29	17.5
9 − 12	12.4	11.5	20	12.0
13 − 28	20.0	21.3	34	20.5

attend in the first few weeks, it is a matter of individual preference. Nevertheless most newcomers are told to 'keep coming to the meetings' a 'friendly injunction' based on the experience of 'the great majority of AAs who find that the quality of their sobriety suffers when they stay away from meetings too long' (*44 Questions*, 1952a).

Alcoholics Anonymous has developed a complex set of procedures for handling a 'new face' at one of its meetings. This involves the whole group in being 'aware' of the newcomer's presence and directing the meeting in such a way as to make it understandable to him. The General Secretary described the process:

It is a group responsibility. One knows a strange face automatically among regular attending members of a meeting. Now this is not one individual's responsibility to welcome that person . . . but the nearest to the door. . . It's easy, just the outstretched hand, 'My name's Bill. I'm an alcoholic'. If he doesn't know anything about AA he will probably say, 'My name is John Smith, I come from such and such a town'. 'All right, John, not interested in your last name and where you come from. Is this your first meeting?' You've established a relationship. Now depending on the group and how it operates, you may find it's more suitable that the member goes outside the meeting room into the passage or another room and has a little private chat with one or two members and they have a little separate meeting . . . '

After this the member may come into the main meeting which will be changed to accommodate him. As long as the chairman, or whoever is speaking, is aware that there *is* a new member he will 'start at the beginning with basics', without letting the new member know this is done specifically for him.

Another opportunity for drawing in the newcomer occurs at the end of the final part of the meeting after the Serenity Prayer:

God grant me the serenity
To accept the things I cannot change
The courage to change the things I can
And the wisdom to know the difference

when people congregate for coffee, refreshments and 'more talking'. 'It's a good time for talking to people', said Mary, 'especially if you've got any newcomers. You can converge on them and make sure they are welcome'.

Stuart Henry wrote the following brief comment immediately after his first visit to an AA meeting at the beginning of the present study of AA. It describes what happened to him and how he was reacted to as a newcomer.

A Report on the 'Open Meeting' at W. 3 November 1975

Approximately thirty people present. Two speakers behind a table, the rest in a circle sitting facing the table. I joined audience.

Stories. I noticed a characteristic style of presentation of 'the story'. It involves continually closing one's eyes and then opening them, some-times pausing with eyes closed, sometimes talking with eyes closed, always talking slowly in a controlled way and seriously. Also apparent is the manner of delivery, i.e. repeating lines so as to add emphasis. It would appear that there may be a learned 'art' of giving a biographical account.

It would be interesting to know if the speaker tells the same story each time he gives his account. Why are certain incidents selected to be told and others not selected? Are different elements drawn on on other occasions, if so, why and what determines this?

Seriousness among speakers and listeners was very evident during the giving of an account. Members relaxed between accounts and after whole story-telling process was over at 'coffee time'.

Members' reaction to stories is to pick out certain pieces and say why they are relevant to them and to elaborate them or emphasise certain points and work in some of their own story. Interestingly no criticism is offered of others' stories only of 'self of old'. When the speaker has finished there is silence until someone else introduces themselves. The pressure to speak is similar to a seminar situation.

After a pause sustained for a longer period one of the two speakers at the table called on one of the members to give the reading which is a section from the 'Big Book'. This is followed by the prayer which appears to close the formal part of the meeting.

The second half of the meeting continues with a collection and with making various announcements. Tea is served and members meet one another.

Collection. The collection was interesting. It is up to the individual how much he puts in the pot. The pot didn't arrive at me (or was deliberately passed to avoid me). I suspect that it was deliberate. Perhaps this is so for new members. I found out later that I was clearly taken to be a new member.

Interaction with Members. I followed up one of the announcements about the start of a new group at Sidcup and collected a notice. I went back and sat down. I was alone for about three to five minutes then a man on my right, who had been sitting there all evening, started a conversation based on the map which I had collected, showing how to get to the Sidcup meeting. He said, 'I see you've got a map of our new group there'. I replied, 'Yes, it's nearer to where I live' and I expressed surprise that there were not more groups locally. He defended AA saying that there were quite a few and listed Beckenham, Bromley, Blackheath, and Greenwich. At this point another member, who had responded to one of the speakers earlier in the meeting, came over. He asked, 'You're new here, aren't you? I haven't seen you before'. He was the member who had (possibly) deliberately passed the collection to someone who was next to me and indicated it should move away from me. I thought it time to reveal where I was from and explained that I was at the ARU doing research into AA. Meanwhile, I had been given a cup of tea by another member who'd then melted away. Another member pulled a chair up alongside me and listened. When the second member heard I was at the Maudsley he asked if I knew certain people. I said I didn't because we were a separate unit. He proceeded to tell me about how the Bethlem Psychiatry Unit was 'doing it all wrong' attempting to reintroduce controlled drinking. He was quite aggressive about this. The first member agreed with him. The third man, who was hard of hearing, and possibly thinking about what he was going to say, started talking. He asked if I knew how to get to the new group and went into vast detail about how I should get there. (He may be useful to ask how a new group is set up.) He got the premises and was pressing for this new group in Bexley.

I talked again with member number two about Selsey (the weekend convention) and how good it was. He said how everyone was enjoying themselves without alcohol. I got the impression that he was trying to probe me and that he was making rapid judgements.

G. from Al-Anon, who I met at Selsey, came across and greeted me with great jubilation. I was reintroduced to member two but he was now involved with something else and seemed to have lost interest.

Interesting to examine these events in the light of their belief that I was seen as a newcomer. After an initial pause there was a rush to see me and to get me involved. The first member seemed to get forced out by the second and the third was waiting to work a flanker by carrying me off to a new group. This raises the question of how frequently newcomers appear and whether there is competition to twelfth step and sponsor them.

Sponsorship. Member two told me a little about sponsorship. He said that when people come, at first they might not find anything in what is said. The sponsor might suggest that he tries another group: 'I usually do. I suggest they get around to two or three different meetings, then they're sure to find somebody there who looks the same as them even if they're not, and that's a start'.
Meeting closed at 10.15.

The AA group attends so closely to the newcomer not only because it wants him to understand and take advantage of the benefits of the fellowship but because a new member is the lifeblood of AA. 'This is the fellow that's going to keep me sober tomorrow'. As one member put it:

The one who arrives, say he's never been to a meeting before. He's the most important person in the room. I tend to aim it at them and bring in things that they may be able to understand. It's not a matter of pulling out the stops. I just speak more to them, so that they can identify.

But it is not always so straightforward. Newcomers have to be controlled as well as encouraged. When a newcomer asks a question this can be seen, on the one hand, as a good sign and as an essential part of the process of identification with the established member's experiences. On the other hand a newcomer's questions can be defined, in some situations, as 'interruptions' that are likely to 'disrupt' or 'threaten' the meeting. Steve remembered one such occasion very clearly:

> There was a newcomer, the Colonel, and he kept interrupting and I ended up walking out. . . . I said, 'Fuck the lot of you'. It was nothing really . . . but he kept coming in and talking and interrupting. I thought, 'Shut your bloody trap'. I said, 'I was told to take the cotton wool out of my ears and put it in my mouth', which he didn't like. He said, 'Are you being sarcastic?' and I ended up going. The next week, the Secretary there had a go at him. I didn't go that week. Anyway, somebody else had a go at him and he walked out. I don't know whether he's still around or not. He hasn't been seen since, I don't think.

Whether or not 'the Colonel' went back again at some time in the future is unknown. He may, of course, have gone to another group which was better able to handle his 'interruptions'. He may, in any case, have been in the process of going to as many meetings as possible, which AA recommend to newcomers, in order to find a group which is congenial. It is not just newcomers, however, who feel the need to go to more than one meeting a week. In fact, as Table 2.5 shows, almost seventy per cent of the current membership have been to an average of more than one meeting a week in the past month, even those people

Table 2.5: Attendance in the Past 4 Weeks

Number of *Meetings* Attended	Years of AA Membership > 6	6 or more	Number of *Groups* Attended	Years of AA Membership > 6	6 or more
1 – 4	31.0	34.5	1	28.3	29.3
5 – 8	24.8	31.0	2	21.2	17.2
9 – 12	25.7	19.0	3	18.6	25.9
13 – 28	18.5	15.5	4 or more	31.9	27.6

who have been in the fellowship for six years or more. Not only do AA members go to more than one meeting a week but they also go to meetings of different groups. As we can see from the right hand side of Table 2.5, seventy per cent of current members, including those who have been members for six years or more, had attended at least two different groups in the month prior to the survey, while thirty per cent had been to four or more different groups.

Edwards's (1967) study of AA in 1964 revealed that the average length of time that members had been in the fellowship was 4.0 years. By the time the AA General Service Board in London conducted its national survey in 1972 this figure had risen to 4.7 years. In the 1976 study it was 5.3 years. It was also clear from the 1976 survey, however, that AA membership is not a continuous matter for many people. In fact, as Table 2.6 shows, just over forty per cent of current members had 'dropped out' at some time; many of them more than once. The most typical 'drop out' period was from between three and six months although some people dropped out for just a couple of weeks and a few for over five years. Almost ninety per cent of those who dropped out said that they drank heavily during the time that they were outside the fellowship.

Table 2.6: 'Dropping Out' and Length of Time in AA

| 'Dropped Out' | Years of AA Membership | | | Total | |
	< 2 %	2 < 6 %	6 or more %	N	%
Never	78.7	55.1	43.1	100	59.5
Once	18.0	38.8	19.0	41	24.4
More than once	3.3	6.1	37.9	27	16.1

While many members of AA 'drop out' and then go back, many other people go to one AA meeting or even a number of meetings and then leave with the very firm intention of never going back. In the survey of fifty out-patient alcoholics from the Maudsley Hospital thirty-two had gone to a number of AA meetings. Of these only three still considered themselves members of AA while only two of the other twenty-nine thought that they would ever go back. Some of these were put off right from the first meeting by the depressive surroundings 'the steel tube chairs and bare floors' or by the uncongenial· 'atmosphere'.

They weren't my type of people.
Even with the hand-shaking and welcoming I didn't feel accepted.
Some people at AA want to be gaffers. There are people who
believe in God and people who don't believe in God and people
who think they are God.

The biggest problem for those newcomers who went to AA but did
not 'take' to it was their inability to identify with the stories which
were being told. As John put it:

It depresses me. The whole idea's a good thing, I think, but the
meetings themselves depress me. I used to feel more depressed
when I came out of AA than I did when I went in. It's the thought
of all this 'My name's Bert and I'm an alcoholic. I've done this and
I've done that and I've done the other'.

It was not that John did not 'identify' with the stories, he did. But he
wanted something more than that:

As I said before, it's just the same story. 'My name is Fred I'm an
alcoholic. I fell down in the gutter'. I've done the same. I've done
the same as Mary and Alison and all the rest of the people. I
went to the pub and couldn't hold the drink. I ended up
interrupting other people's conversations. I didn't know what I
was doing. It's all the same story. I know and I accept what I am.
I can never be a social drinker. I accept this. But I don't want to
hear it every day. I want to do something else.

For Andrew, another person who didn't find AA the answer, the
difficulty was in identifying with the *successes* in AA:

S.H.   Why didn't you go back to AA rather than go back to
         the booze?
Andrew   I think I did try. I went to a few meetings at Acton, though
         I was pretty drunk. It boils down to that I think I've seen
         too many successes in AA. And I've always seen myself as
         a failure.
S.H.   But you also see the failures in AA.
Andrew   Yes *you* see the failures and *I've* seen the successes. For me
         the successes made up for more than the failures. . .

Becoming a Member

It is always difficult to pinpoint the time at which a newcomer becomes
a member. To outsiders it often seems as though anyone who goes to a
meeting is a member but, as we have seen earlier, many people who go
to meetings certainly do not feel that they belong and many others go to
one meeting and do not return to the group. Becoming a member of a
self-help group involves more than length of service. Being a member
means belonging and being a part. In order for the newcomer to stand
any chance of becoming a member in this sense it is essential to feel
that the group and its activities are relevant to him and his problems.
Some newcomers find something of value at their first meeting from
the fact that people seemed to be making out. 'I can't tell you what
was said. The words are unimportant. But what I took from the room
was seven or eight guys who were clean, respectable, from all walks of
life, who had made it. It gave me hope that I could do it too'.

Others are not so fortunate. They may not feel a real part of the
fellowship until they have gone to a great many meetings, told their
story a large number of times, developed a long-lasting relationship
with a sponsor and been on a twelfth step call. Twelfth Stepping
someone else is, for many members, a real turning point in their AA
career. It is the time when they feel that they belong enough to 'carry
the message'. For many people, this is when they really begin to think
of themselves as members.

3 SHARING THE PROBLEM

> AA's major source of appeal for new members is shared
> experience. AA meetings provide the context of a supportive
> peer group. (Bean 1975)

The first time that a potential member walks into an AA group meeting
they are, in effect, saying that they think they *may* have something in
common with the people who are present. They may have something to
share. This chapter discusses what sharing means in the context of AA
and outlines what is shared.

Wootton (1977) points out that while the word 'sharing' is usually
used to refer to the distribution of objects, it is also used in relation to
the distribution of information, such as sharing secrets, ideas or
experiences. He then goes on to distinguish two kinds of information
sharing. First, there is information given by someone about themselves
when they talk of their past and present life, activities and experiences.
Second there is the information provided by a person that is 'the same
as' that provided by other people. Sharing this second kind of information is more commonly known as 'identifying'. Recognising something as 'the same as' one's own experience was seen, in the previous
chapter, to be a crucial aspect of a successful Twelfth Stepping contact.
This chapter outlines other aspects of sharing which underlie the self-
help process of Alcoholics Anonymous.

'Sharing' is a word which is frequently heard at AA meetings and
recurs many times in the AA literature. The journal of AA in England
and Wales is *Share* and edited by 'The Sharers', while the correspondence section is called 'Sharing by Letter' and has the following
introduction.

> Readers of this magazine often feel like commenting on some-
> thing they have read in its pages, or putting forward some thought
> or opinion that is of shorter length than an article. We welcome
> your sharing at all times.

Clearly, sharing is an important aspect of AA, but what does it
mean? The AA newsletter, *Box 514* (1975), asked the question this
way:

Sharing is truly more than a word. . . Perhaps we should from time to time re-examine what we really mean by sharing — and what it is we are offering to share. What, in other words, is the reality behind the symbolic concept of sharing? What do we really mean, for example, when we say that we share our 'experience, strength and hope?' The problem is not that it is inaccurate to say that we are offering experience, strength and hope — but that the words alone fail to convey the total sense of what we are offering.

For Alcoholics Anonymous, and other self-help groups, 'the symbolic concept of sharing' is translated into action in terms of two closely interrelated processes of deconstruction and reconstruction. Deconstruction refers to the process of taking apart and handling the various parts of the particular problem or set of problems which is the group's concern. Reconstruction refers to the process of putting together a new set of relationships and a new way of everyday life. These two processes make up the activity of self-help and form the substance of the 'symbolic concept of sharing'.

Alcoholism as 'The Problem'

Before a problem can be shared, it has to be defined. And the question of what constitutes the problem is not as straightforward an idea as it might appear from the outside. As was pointed out in the previous chapter a potential member has, at some stage, to identify with the kind of problems which are being presented by a Twelfth Stepper or with the problems outlined in the AA literature in order to raise the possibility that they may be an alcoholic and that, therefore, Alcoholics Anonymous may have something to offer.

The question of what constitutes alcoholism is a never ending concern of those who treat alcoholism or who contribute to the alcoholism literature. Over the past century there has been a discernible and well-documented shift (Jellinek 1960) from defining alcoholism as primarily a legal or moral problem: ' . . . a sin, heinous and soul-wrecking, whose victims shall not possess the Kingdom of Heaven' (Ireland 1894) to considering it primarily as one of medicine or public health: ' . . . few would deny that it is a condition which belongs to the sphere of the healing professions' (Glatt 1970) or more specifically as: ' . . . a psychological dependence on, or physiological addiction to ethanol manifested by the inability . . . consistently to control either the start of drinking or its termination once started. . . ' (Keller 1960).

But despite this broad shift of emphasis the difficulty of defining alcoholism is readily acknowledged by those who work with, study, treat, help, judge or live with people who consider themselves or are considered by others to have some alcohol-related problem. Listen to Kessel and Walton (1965), for example, as they wrestle with 'the question of definition':

> What is an alcoholic? Without being adequately defined the term is too readily applied to embrace everybody who drinks abnormally. Not all these are alcoholics. Furthermore, there are many different types of alcoholics and many varied patterns of alcoholism. Some define the alcoholic from the vantage point of the sufferer; they name as an alcoholic the person who recognises that he has to stop drinking but cannot do so. Others have focused on the observable consequences of uncontrolled drinking; they define an alcoholic as a person whose drinking has caused increasing problems in his health, his domestic or social life or with his work. Others emphasise the quantity of alcohol consumed and the pattern of the drinking habits; only the man who regularly drinks till he is helpless is an alcoholic from their point of view.

Having so succinctly posed the problem of definition they then attempt to solve it by constructing a classification which distinguishes teetotallers from social drinkers, excessive drinkers, alcoholics, alcohol addicts and chronic alcoholics:

> Some people are *teetotallers*.
> Most people drink moderatly, they may from time to time get drunk. These are *social drinkers*.
> Some people drink excessively, though not necessarily in their own eyes; their excess may show either by the frequency with which they become intoxicated or by the social, economic, or medical consequences of their continued intake of alcohol. These are *excessive drinkers*. . .
> *Alcoholics* are people with a disease that can be defined in medical terms and requires a proper regime of treatment. Alcoholics are addicted to alcohol. *Alcohol addicts* are unable spontaneously to give up drinking. Though they may go without a drink for a few days, or sometimes for even longer periods, inevitably they revert. The greater the need to stop drinking, the more difficult do they find it to do so. . .
> Most alcoholics proceed to a stage where their brains or their

bodies have been so harmed by alcohol that the effects persist even when they are not drinking. This stage may be reached by some excessive drinkers who had not manifested addiction. It is called *chronic alcoholism*. The term should only be applied when the body has been physically damaged by alcohol.

This classificatory scheme is similar to many others in the academic and professional literature. Some are based on clinical insight and experience (Glatt 1970) and others on systematic abstractions from case histories (Jellinek 1946). But, unfortunately, attempts to construct universally applicable definitions have been rather unsuccessful. This is hardly surprising since any definition or description which purported to incorporate the physiological, biochemical, psychological, legal, moral, religious nature of the phenomenon; the process of its development and likely prognosis; the indications for help or treatment; together with its effects upon the individual and the wider society, is likely to be either totally incomprehensible or of such generality as to bear no meaningful relationship to the social world. Yet, since the many and varied features listed above have all at some time or other been cited as essential components of definitions of alcoholism, the search for a universal, all-purpose definition will no doubt continue. And it is easy to understand why. For clinicians and other helping professionals often feel unable to proceed unless they can match cases to a classification which implies certain therapeutic or helping procedures. As Kessel and Walton (1965) put it:

> To classify a particular drinker may not be easy, yet it is essential if he is to be helped. We cannot properly proceed until we know whether he is a social drinker, an excessive drinker, an excessive drinker with problems, an alcoholic (i.e. an alcohol addict), or has reached the further stage of chronic alcoholism.

But the mere construction of general wide-ranging definitions of alcoholism does not really advance our understanding of particular patterns of alcohol consumption or the way in which associated problems are defined or handled by particular groups of people. In order to throw light on these questions we must not take for granted at the outset what 'alcoholism', or 'drinking problem', or 'being an alcoholic' is. What is needed instead is an understanding of what these things mean to particular people in particular situations. Such an approach is especially necessary in the discussion of drinking and alcoholism when the medical, psychological, physiological and biochemical bases for regarding someone as an alcoholic are so open to dispute.

Given all this, what is Alcoholics Anonymous's view of alcoholism? Although AA talk of alcoholism and its causes, their approach to the nature of the problem 'challenges the conventional medical, psychological and sociological concepts of causation' and 'ignores the findings and questions of specialists in these fields' (Thune 1977). This does not mean that AA does its own scientific research and holds, for example, a unique theory of the biochemistry of alcohol ingestion or the structure of an alcoholic predisposed personality. The search for causes in these terms is quite outside AA's concern. Alcoholics Anonymous has a clear and simple model of alcoholism which it holds and propagates. It is not a model which is based on scientific research, however, but on the collected experience of the early members and their interpretation of what the nature of their shared problem must be like.

Like all therapeutic systems AA faces the twin problems of diagnosis and treatment. That is, they have statements to make about both, and are concerned about both in relation to any particular person. But although the basic AA position is that alcoholism is an illness there is no attempt to identify signs of illness in an individual and then treat them. The success of the programme depends on whether the individual can diagnose himself as an alcoholic. And central to this is helping the potential member to understand his basic 'being' as alcoholic rather than as normal and non alcoholic. For AA, alcoholism is a matter of being rather than having. The AA member '*is* an alcoholic' rather than 'a person who *has* alcoholism'.

Being an alcoholic means first of all that one is 'physically allergic' to drink. Second, the alcoholic is held to possess an 'alcoholic personality' described as immature and self-centred. Third, he is 'spiritually sick'; his naively egotistical and self-centred personality prevents any but the most artificial and superficial relations to others or to a 'higher power'.

Bean (1975) has stressed how AA's view of allergy differs from conventional medical understanding: 'The apparent meaning here is that when a person takes a drink it inevitably leads to more'. The 'uniqueness' of the allergy has been described by one AA member (L.C. 1976) in the following terms.

The allergy to alcohol is perhaps unique in that we develop this craving for the thing that harms us. Allergy to strawberries or fish doesn't lead to a craving for them; we shun them and we are mentally sane enough to see that we remain well if we don't eat them. But some of us, even when the nature of an allergy is pointed out, still persist in drinking; and this extraordinary mental obsession with drink lingers on long after the actual physical craving has gone.

Trice and Roman (1970) have concluded that the 'substance of the allergy concept is that those who become alcoholics possess a physiological allergy such that their addiction is predetermined even before they take their first drink'. In short, the AA position is that alcoholics, for some unknown reason, are not as other people. But, as L.C. (1976) made very clear, it is not just an illness which one 'has', it is 'an illness of the whole person. It embraces the physical, having an effect on the brain. The whole thinking goes haywire. This is mental and it has an effect on the spiritual side of the human being'.

Given this view of the threefold nature of alcoholism as a defect of being, the Alcoholics Anonymous programme is geared to changing the alcoholic's total lifestyle or mode of being and action in the world, within which the consumption of alcohol is only one part. Paradoxically, though, while the elimination of drinking is an indispensable first concern this is not the fundamental component of the programme. Rather, it is a first step before altering other, more basic, aspects of the overall defective lifestyle.

Fixing initially on some specific, easily definable and simple task, while at the same time preparing the member for a fundamental change in his way of life is a familiar feature of many self-help groups. Of all the problems which women face in today's world, for example, in relation to employment, housing, law, interpersonal relationships and so on it is significant that the one thing which many women's health groups take to be of great importance is to inspect one's cervix with a speculum. In many groups this is an initiation task which signals membership and commitment to the group in particular and the movement in general. Although it is traumatic for some women, and an extremely significant gesture of one's determination to wrest back control over one's body, it is an extremely simple task compared with many others which could be envisaged, such as changing the tax laws or rules about property or rights in relation to children or abortion. But the significance of the act is essential. Like giving up drinking it is something which anyone can do and thus immediately become a person who can control one's self — one's life and thus one's destiny. The maintenance of this new found position of strength is then the task of the group. In women's groups it is maintaining the individual as a person who can take control over her own life. In the AA group it is maintaining the individual as a person who can live a sober life without alcohol.

One central problem which members face in AA is the relationship between alcohol and alcoholism as popularly understood and as conceptualised within the group. Whereas society takes alcohol and the alcoholic to be irrevocably linked, the fellowship insists on their separation. AA argues that an individual is an alcoholic whether or not he drinks and, indeed, that his behaviour may be that of a typical alcoholic even if he has not had a drink for years. This means, of course, that for the alcoholic his condition is lifelong and so the help and support he gets from AA must be lifelong also. The aim is to establish and maintain alcoholics in an alcohol-free life.

Since there is no way in which the alcoholic will ever stop being an alcoholic, Alcoholics Anonymous never look for elaborate causal theories or even for the particular causes of particular people's problems. That, for them, would be a waste of time since, whatever the cause, the main task is to enable the drinker to recognise that he is 'an alcoholic' and then to help him to manage that fact within the context of AA. And the whole programme and the nature of the relationships between members is based on this particular conception of the nature of alcoholism as an illness with three components which in sum add up to making alcoholism a defect of being rather than something which one has.

Deconstructing the Problem

The range of difficulties which go to make up any individual's alcohol 'problem' can be very wide. Problems of interpersonal relations, loss of job, violence, physical illness, trouble with the police, severe depression and many more. This is a feature of many of the problems which are taken to self-help groups. They are often multiple, longstanding, and seen to be affecting almost every aspect of the individual's personal, interpersonal and wider social life.

The task of the self-help group is then to initiate the processes of deconstructing the overall problem. And, paradoxically perhaps, the first stage of deconstructing the problem, in many self-help groups, is to get the individual to concentrate on it, to admit that they really are 'an alcoholic', 'a child abuser', 'a fatty', 'a compulsive gambler' or whatever is the focus of the group's concern. The process of concentrating on 'the' real problem among all the problems that one faces begins, of course, when the person with the problem first thinks of approaching a particular group. At that stage they are admitting to themselves the possibility that their 'real' problem is, for example, alcoholism. The next step in the process of taking on the identity of an alcoholic or a compulsive gambler is to go through the door of a group meeting. As Parents Anonymous say,

> Going to a PA chapter is a way a person says 'I'm here because I have a child abuse problem'. For some people it may be extremely difficult. However, the sooner you can share the nature of your concern for the problem, the sooner other members will be able to relate to you in ways that will offer direct assistance in helping you solve your individual circumstances.

The third and particularly important part of concentrating on the problem is to make a public declaration that you accept that you are whatever is the group's concern. Gamblers Anonymous and Parents Anonymous, among many, have adopted the simple Alcoholics Anonymous formula of making it quite natural to begin any formal contribution to a meeting with the words 'My name is X and I am an alcoholic'. Parents Anonymous begin 'My name is Y and I've got problems as a parent and I want help. My problem shows itself in the form of . . . [whatever form of abuse has been shown; verbal, emotional, physical, sexual or neglect]'.

Once the public declaration has been made the sense of relief can be enormous. Many members say that the relief on publicly sharing the problem is their single most important experience. Knowing that you are neither 'alone' nor 'unique' has been described among other things as heartening, gladdening, reassuring and comforting. As time goes on the declarations contain other functions. As Griffith Edwards (1964) put it: 'To be able to say "I'm an alcoholic" without embarrassment, and perhaps sometimes it seems even with a certain implication of pride, is the badge of the AA member'.

In addition to relief and pride the declaration at an AA meeting that the member is an alcoholic means also that he is stuck publicly with the persona of 'an alcoholic' and all that that means to AA. It means that he has publicly accepted that he is not as other men, that his alcoholism is an essential part of him which will never change, but that he is making a contract to change other parts of his life to cope with the fact of being an alcoholic and in the hope of remaining for the rest of his life a sober alcoholic. So buried in the declaration and being known as an

alcoholic in AA's terms, is the acceptance of a strand of permanence —
being an alcoholic — and a commitment to change — never drinking
again, making reparation, and building up a new sober life.

Talking and Stories

As anyone who has ever been in contact with AA members will know,
talking is the one thing that AA members do more than anything else.
Everybody talks in AA, and everybody loves it. When members were
asked to say what they got most out of in the AA meeting it was
'talks and stories' and 'taking part in discussion groups'. As Table 3.1
shows, official AA business was well down the list.

Table 3.1: Helpfulness of Different Parts of AA Meetings

Part of the Meeting (N = 171)	Very Helpful %	Fairly Helpful %	Not Helpful At All %
Hearing talks and stories	75.0	22.0	3.0
Discussion groups	75.0	14.9	10.1
Discussion after prayer	66.0	32.0	2.0
Giving talks and stories	64.7	26.6	8.7
Discussion before meeting	51.7	40.6	7.7
Official AA business	30.2	44.4	25.4

It is not surprising, then, that members were much more likely to have
read *Share*, the AA journal, which is full of 'members' stories', than
Box 514, the newsletter from the General Service Office.

Talking is the mechanism of change in AA. Bill, the AA General
Secretary stressed its importance.

> All we can hope to do, by talking about a person's experience is
> change his attitude. . . Who am I to say he is wrong? I must be
> tolerant and accept that this is how he is thinking. It may be a
> barrier to his recovery and all I can hope to do is influence his
> thinking and outlook . . . by talking. You kick a ball around long
> enough and you'll have a game, won't you? Talk, talk, talk and
> because you talk you start a man thinking.

For an AA member the opportunities for talking are almost limitless.
AA formal meetings, for example, are built around the core activity of

members exchanging experiences with each other. The style of the talking depends on the kind of meeting, whether it is a 'discussion', 'speaker' or 'open' meeting. Discussion meetings usually begin with someone reading aloud from the AA literature and then inviting comments and experiences from other members. At speaker meetings, three or four members, often from another AA group, each stand up and speak for about half an hour on a particular theme related to their drinking experiences and recovery from alcoholism. An open meeting is similar to a speaker meeting except that non-AA members are allowed to attend.

Surrounding the formal part of any AA meeting there are numerous occasions for informal talk between members, with newcomers or with sponsors: prior to the start of a meeting, during coffee and after the formal meeting has been closed. These informal talking sessions enable newcomers to be welcomed in a more personal way than is possible during the full meeting. They also permit a member to talk to his sponsor about intimate, private or detailed problems that would be irrelevant to the formal meetings.

> You can talk to one person about things that you can't talk about at a meeting. You can talk about so much in a meeting but there are some things . . . like you've got a private life, I've got one, we've all got one. See, that's the idea really of a sponsor . . . Like Joe, we'll talk about different things that we can't talk about at a meeting.

In addition to talking at meetings there are several other particular kinds of talking, such as talking on a Twelfth Step call, talking at AA conferences and conventions, talking about AA's official business, or talking about AA to outside organisations such as schools, hospitals or the Women's Institute. Important too, is the talking which goes on between AA members either over the telephone or when they meet each other outside formal AA functions; at one another's homes, at work, and on a whole range of social, sporting and leisure occasions.

Since most kinds of talking are represented at a routine AA meeting a sample of members were asked whether they had ever spoken at a meeting. Less than two per cent said that they had never said anything, although a further seven per cent admitted hardly speaking at all. There is a negligible difference between men and women in respect of talking, with women speaking slightly less regularly than men. The length of time that a member has been in the fellowship does seem to affect the frequency with which members speak at meetings. As might be expected, those who have been in AA for a relatively short time do not speak as regularly as those who have been AA members for longer periods. However, as we can see from Table 3.2, after the peak between four and six years in the fellowship, the regularity with which members talk at a meeting begins to decline.

Table 3.2: Speaking at a Meeting and Length of Time in AA

Frequency of Speaking	Under 1 %	1–2 %	Years in AA 2–4 %	4–6 %	6–10 %	Over 10 %	Total N	%
Regularly	41.7	53.8	64.3	82.6	70.4	71.0	107	62.5
Occasionally	38.9	42.3	25.0	17.4	22.2	22.6	49	28.7
Hardly at all	13.9	3.8	10.7	0	7.4	3.2	12	7.0
Never	5.6	0	0	0	0	3.2	3	1.8

Although so few members have never spoken at an AA meeting many of them find it very difficult to do so the first time. One member described how he had hidden himself away in his bed-sitter and rarely gone out to see or talk to anyone: 'I'd become like a recluse'. Then he began going to AA and for months he never said a word to anyone.

At first when I went to AA I was told to listen. Well, as it was, I couldn't speak anyway because I was so scared. They got me by the bloke in the chair saying, 'How are you tonight?' and I'd say, 'Eh, what?' and I had to say a little something. That's how I started to speak. But I'd felt very guilty for a long time because I wasn't contributing. People have said it was pride or self-respect. I was just plain scared of having to talk and knowing what to say. It always seemed as though somebody else had said it.

At that time he had not recognised that an essential part of AA talking is saying things which are 'the same as everybody else'. That is how the sharing part of the self-help process of AA is demonstrating itself. People can recognise incidents, feelings and experiences and identify with someone who clearly understands what it is like to have 'the problem'.

The content of the talking which takes place in any of the different aspects of an AA meeting is specific enough to include particular difficulties such as how to avoid drinking, and yet at the same time sufficiently accommodating to accept accounts of almost any aspect of a person's day-to-day living problems. Nevertheless, most AA talk usually relates to problems associated with drinking or not drinking. Personal stories make up the major proportion of AA's basic book, *Alcoholics Anonymous* (1939). In addition, no matter how informal is the forum for talking, personal stories are usually the main vehicle for sharing information and experience within the fellowship. An analysis of the talk of personal stories permits us to understand a great deal about talk in AA.

The format for telling personal stories is given by example in the AA literature and is easily learned by someone attending an AA meeting. Put simply, it requires a person to describe how he began drinking, his experiences when drunk, the effects of his drinking on himself and others, what happened to him when he came to AA and what he has been like since joining the fellowship.

Although telling one's story is a very familiar part of AA group activity, not everyone does it. Eighteen per cent of current members had never told their story and, as can be seen from Table 3.3, women were less likely to have told their story than men. It is also evident from Table 3.3 that, apart from newcomers, the likelihood of someone telling their story was unrelated to a member's time in the fellowship. In fact, of those who had been in the fellowship for six years or more, twelve per cent had never told their story. This suggests that for some members, at least, telling personal stories is not an essential part of staying in AA.

Table 3.3: Telling Personal Stories, Sex and Length of Time in AA

Ever told story	Years in AA						Sex		Total	
	Under 1 %	1–2 %	2–4 %	4–6 %	6–10 %	Over 10 %	Men %	Women %	N	%
Yes	61.1	80.8	89.3	91.3	88.9	87.1	88.0	72.6	140	81.9
No	38.9	19.2	10.7	8.7	11.1	12.9	12.0	27.4	31	18.1

Nevertheless, among those with long-standing membership, as Table 3.4 shows, there is an association between not telling one's story and dropping out.

Most of the eighteen per cent of members who had never told their stories gave reasons for not doing so. Both men and women who had been in AA under one year accounted for not telling their story in terms

Table 3.4: Dropping out and telling Personal Stories among Those with 6+ years of Membership

| | Told Story | | | Total |
Dropped Out	Yes %	No %	N	%
Never	45.1	28.6	25	43.1
Once	19.6	14.3	11	19.0
More than once	35.3	57.1	22	37.9

of: not being in the fellowship long enough; being a 'new member'; and having 'not been sober long enough'. Most of these members said they lacked confidence and were still 'too nervous' to tell their story. Many of those who had been in AA for between one and two years felt they were 'still not ready'. One member said she was 'afraid of getting it wrong and boring people'. Two other members said that no one told their whole story at a meeting and another member said that he had told his story to his sponsor but not to the group at the meeting. Of the members who had been in the fellowship longer than four years and who had still not told their story, some were just 'shy'. One member felt that his story was only 'ordinary' and another felt he could say all that was necessary in five minutes. One member felt that 'reticence, embarrassment and a great deal of shame' prevented him from telling his story.

Of current members who had told their story, almost seventy per cent had told it within six months of going to AA for the first time. After the first year in the fellowship, the regularity with which members tell their story is unaffected by their length of time in AA, although it does vary between the sexes. As Table 3.5 shows, of those members who had told their story in the past year, men told it more regularly than women.

A core feature of the deconstruction process of Alcoholics Anonymous is the way in which the member's past drinking experience is handled. Rather than being denied or rejected or ignored the member's drinking experience is brought out into the open and made the focus of attention: 'It is discussed lovingly and rather than attempt to exorcise its memory, the members reverently and ritually mourn it. Its past importance in the alcoholic's life is accepted as valid and comprehensible' (Bean 1975). And it is in the member's story that the drinking experience is presented. The public presentation of the personal

Table 3.5: Told Story in the Past Year

Number of Times Story Told in Past Year	Men %	Women %	N	Total %
Never	14.1	27.4	31	19.3
Once or twice	19.2	25.8	35	21.7
Three or four times	22.2	22.6	36	22.4
Five times or more	44.5	24.2	59	36.6

story is at the heart of the process of changing the member's perception of himself – his past, his worth and his place in the world. The drinking story becomes a thing to be valued since, rather than being merely a catalogue of past ills and evils, it can be put to use for the benefit of others.

The crucial value of personal stories for others is the opportunity they provide for members to 'identify'. Identification has been defined by Bean (1975) as meaning to 'empathise in reverse, to feel that what the speaker experienced can be meaningful to yourself and feel what he felt, not so that you can better understand him, but so that you can accept yourself'. One AA member described identification as 'the different things that I may have done or felt which may provoke others to say, "Oh, I've done this" '. However as Edwards *et al* . (1967) have pointed out in an earlier study of the fellowship, 'Identification . . . is not necessarily just with any one established member so much as with fragments of a whole series of life histories which are synthesized into identification with the group ideal'. Nevertheless, some people do want a particular person to identify with who, in turn, would identify with them. As Andrew said, 'I'm going to meet the right person one day and think, "Christ, you're me". I know he's there somewhere. It's only through going to AA meetings that I'm going to discover him. He could be a pillar to me and I could be a pillar to him'.

While it is easy to learn the format of story-telling, it is often difficult for some people to understand what is meant by it. Newcomers may, at first, see it merely as impression management to qualify them as a member, and may over-dramatize their own experiences to compete with others.

When I was able to talk at meetings I used to think 'What can I come out with?' I'd always thought that you'd got to say the right sort of things to impress people. You've got to impress everybody.

And I even went to some meetings where the stories were so
horrific that I thought of tarting mine up. Mine seemed so dull and I
thought it was very bad. I thought, 'This is awful, you've got to do
better than that'. So in the beginning I used to come out with the
little gems. Things to bring the house down, you know, laughter,
all the escapades I got up to. See I always thought that you'd got
to identify with the speaker, to say similar to what he said. If
he'd said 'Pigs fly', well I'd have to come and say I agreed. But I've
learnt to speak as I feel, to be honest.

It can be seen in Table 3.6 that approximately half of the members
gained something from *all* stories they heard and men found them
more helpful than did women. Nevertheless, almost all of the members
said that they always listened to stories *until* they found something
useful. Others pointed out that all stories give reminders of what they
were like and could be like again, which, said one member, 'keeps us
on our toes'. Another member said that even having to listen to long,
boring details taught tolerance, and so was useful from this point of
view.

Table 3.6: Usefulness of hearing Personal Stories

Usefulness of Stories	Men %	Women %	Total N	%
Gain something from all stories	53.7	35.5	80	47.1
Gain something from 75% of stories	27.8	38.7	54	31.8
Gain something from 50% of stories	14.8	14.5	25	14.6
Gain something from 25% of stories	3.7	11.3	11	6.5

However, a substantial majority, sixty nine per cent of members,
said that there were things that they did not find helpful in other
people's stories. To some people, of course, the repetition of the story
with its focus on the drinking experience is boring, or irritating. John
felt it was depressing:

It depresses me. The whole idea's a good thing, I think, but the
meetings themselves depress me. . . It's all the bloody same. It was a
repeat. In the group I was in you began to memorise everybody's
history and it just depressed me.

and without much point:

> I could never see the point of discussing. . . All they talked about
> was the degradation that they went down to which we've all done.
> But it just didn't do anything for me.

Three themes of criticism recurred. The first referred to 'drunkalogues'; when a speaker dwells on his past drinking history, talking
at great length and giving repeated 'blow by blow' details of 'what,
when, where and how they drank', 'the names of pubs and the days of
the week'. Many members found these to be monotonous, laborious,
boring, and having a 'sameness' which was unhelpful. A related aspect
that members did not like was stories that had a 'negative attitude'
towards recovery. In these, members describe their drinking behaviour
before joining AA but give no emphasis to their improvement since
coming to the fellowship. The third major criticism of other people's
stories was the inclusion of 'irrelevant personal problems'. These
'domestic trivialities', 'war experiences', 'detailed chores' and, as one
member graphically put it, 'the colour of their grandmothers', were
considered to be just part of life and as such not worth talking
about.

It was obviously unhelpful, as several members pointed out, when a
person could not identify in any way with the experiences of the
speaker. This was mentioned by some men of women's stories and
vice-versa. More interestingly various members found it unhelpful
when people 'theorised' or 'philosophised about *why* they became
alcoholics' or when they were seeking causes in their 'childhood
backgrounds'. Similarly, any emphasis on the humour, romance or
enjoyment of drinking was disturbing, as were descriptions of mental
hospitals, prisons or suicides. As one member said, he did not find it
useful to hear 'blood and thunder horror tales'. Especially unhelpful
were stories in which the teller was on an 'ego trip' engaged in 'self-
glorification', 'self-congratulation' or, as one member put it, 'being
Mr AA'.

Finally, certain styles of speaking were felt to be unhelpful, such as
when members were 'being repetitive', 'wandering', 'rambling', talking
too long, or giving too much description. The whole position was
perhaps best summed up by the member who said that stories were
unhelpful when the speaker 'forgot everyone else in the room'.

The survey of AA members indicates that a substantial majority of
members changed their personal stories. Of the 146 members who had

told their stories, just over eighty per cent of both men and women said it had changed since they first told it. However, as can be seen from Table 3.7, women change their story far earlier than men with almost sixty per cent changing it within four years, compared with only thirty-five per cent of men over the same period.

Table 3.7: Time taken for Men and Women to change their Story

Sex	Under 1 %	1–2 %	2–4 %	Over 4 %	N	Total %
Men	10.0	12.5	12.5	65.0	80	67.2
Women	10.3	25.6	23.1	41.0	39	32.8

Since the story is the vehicle for carrying accounts of members' current problems together with their past experiences, the longer active involvement in the fellowship goes on, the more the members' talk moves away from their original problem experience of drinking. The drinking story includes reportable stages of life since joining AA and aspects of life outside AA.

Anyone can come in with whatever is on their minds. . . See, it's not just about alcohol. It's a problem of living and the whole thing is sharing. A year or so back I wanted to buy a house. I was assessed for what I was worth. When it came to it I could barely raise the bloody mortgage. I got in a hell of a state. I dragged that around meetings for a month or so just talking about it. Nobody offered me any money, but it got it out of my system. See, you can talk about anything that is getting you down.

As can be seen from Table 3.8, the emphasis of personal stories changes from drinking to recovery.

The change in emphasis may lead them to change their formal group meeting to one dealing more with recovery and less with drinking problems.

Bill (General Secretary of AA) Again the principle of AA is based on talking and sharing. Obviously, if a group is a group, and let's start on this assumption, it will attract people who have a problem and they will stay and that group will grow in numbers. Now

Table 3.8: The Changes in Members' Stories over Time

Changes	Under 1 %	1–2 %	2–4 %	4–6 %	6–10 %	Over 10 %	N	Total %
			Years in AA					
More honest	25.0	25.0	21.1	9.5	30.0	14.8	24	20.2
'Remember' more details	41.7	20.0	15.8	19.1	5.0	7.4	19	16.0
Less drinking and more recovery as a way of life	25.0	50.0	52.6	61.9	60.0	77.8	69	58.0
Other changes such as more humour, more understanding directed to others	8.3	5.0	10.5	9.5	5.0	0.0	7	5.8

you get to the stage where the group can be large and in fact only a small portion of those people would be able to talk, even if they wanted to. So conference has discussed this one and they say, look here, when you start getting above fifteen in a good group, you are starting to get a little bit unmanageable. You've not got the opportunity for everybody to talk. So when a group starts creeping up to twenty or thirty, it's time to start thinking of forming another group. You're getting, perhaps, people having to travel twenty miles. How about forming a group mid-way between? So this is a divide and grow.

D.R. Since groups are autonomous, their style of working varies obviously from group to group and as groups grow one of the major sort of ways of splitting a group, would be crudely on the more rather than less spiritual dimension. This is a way in which groups have been described as being different. Some more emphasising the spiritual element. Might this be a dimension on which perhaps some of the members want to split off from some of the other members? It wouldn't always just be a business of either location or distance travel or this kind of business.

Bill No, or just size. You can have disagreements.

D.R. Then that would be an opportunity really for one group of people to say well this really is the best way we have found to sort of maintain ourselves so it would be best if we split up.

Bill Yes, but if the motives of the people who start a group up are wrong, that group will fail.

D.R. Yes. What then would be an example of wrong motive?

Bill Personality. That big shot, you know, the old ego coming out again I'm going to have my own bloody group. I'm going to be boss. 'Cos I can't get my own way in this group. So what is happening, the thinking is going wrong.

D.R. But there would be legitimate differences about . . . given that the groups are autonomous, there is the possibility of legitimate differences about the way in which groups, day to day, organise themselves so it would be legitimate disagreement, wouldn't it?

Bill Yes. But these differences cannot be argument or dissension. It can be progress. You may have a group which serves a very useful purpose for the newcomer, keeping to the basic recovery: 'Don't take that first drink today'. You know, this basic stuff. Now a person may perhaps say, 'Well, I've got past this stage, I want something with a little more depth. I want to talk about the steps'. The older, wiser member would say, 'Well, the purpose of this group is, we hope, to help the newcomer. Perhaps you'd like to form a group that would discuss in depth the steps'.

D.R. That was exactly what I meant, really, where there would be a difference of function between the groups — between some groups and other groups, as you say.

Bill Oh, yes, it depends what the members want. Their stage of recovery. You see lots of things in AA evolve, they are not directed. They evolve. Because there is a need it is provided. And this is the good will that exists in AA, and it doesn't mean to say that any one side or any one aspect of AA is wrong. It is always right at some point of time in our recovery. See, there are no bad AA groups from the AA members' point of view, if you appreciate what AA is. Because you know there is a different requirement at different stages of recovery. Now a new member because of immaturity, somebody who doesn't really appreciate what AA is all about, could go to a meeting and it could be say a meeting, that concentrates on discussing the steps and he could say, 'What a load of old baloney this is. What a bloody bad group this is'. But this is because they don't appreciate what is actually happening. The beauty of it is, and this is one of the advantages of our growth, an assortment of different types of groups, different aspects of it. One doesn't have to be restricted. You can go to different groups. You're not a member of one group, and that's the only group you can go to. You are a member of AA and you're entirely free to go to any group which is published in that directory.

It is worth noting that as well as changing the content of their accounts of past experience, and their ways of separating themselves from their own past experience, AA members use a range of other linguistic devices or ways of talking about non-members that cuts them off from the non-alcoholic population. They construct a mutuality of 'we' talk, a private sub-cultural language, which Bean (1975) has said acts as a verbal symbol of group cohesion.

A private AA language helps foster group identification and solidarity. They speak of 'having resentments' bearing a grudge. This is something to be avoided. 'You can't afford resentments if you're alcoholic' . . . Relapses are called 'slips' and 'going out to do more research'. These were all catch phrases, understood by initiates . . . [The meeting room] . . . is usually decorated with banners bearing the mottoes 'First things first', 'Easy does it', and the famous Serenity Prayer.

This AA talk is well recognised by AA members as something different from ordinary talk with outsiders: 'I've talked to you like an ordinary person, not doing AA talk like I would to another AA. You get into the way of switching on to the other. It just becomes automatic.'

Sharing the Problem

Sharing is the basis of the self-help process of Alcoholics Anonymous and other mutual aid groups. On the basis of the literature produced by self-help groups of various kinds, they most typically see themselves as *fellowships*. Great stress is put on the *common* problem, position or circumstance, colloquially expressed as 'being in the same boat'. Being in the same boat means, first of all, understanding the problems of others, that is, 'knowing what it's like'. It is said that only those experiencing the problem can *really* understand. As CARE, the Cancer Aftercare and Rehabilitation Society, put it:

The organisation consists in the main of cancer patients — people who know what it is like to have cancer, who know the problems, mental and social. These people we feel are best fitted to give assistance and help to patients and families before and after treatment.

It is this identification and understanding, based on common experience, which produces the necessary common bond of mutual interest among self-help group members and common desire to do something about their shared problem. And the basic ingredient of this 'doing something' is collectively helping oneself, sharing information and experiences which enable the member to talk himself out of his problem.

First of all, though, as we have seen, it is essential for the member to recognise what the nature of his particular problem is and to concentrate on it. In Alcoholics Anonymous it is necessary to accept that the 'real' problem 'being an alcoholic' is something which is part of the person. It is a defect of being. But on the basis of sharing experience, strength and hope it is possible to contain the problem, make it manageable and, further than that, to put it to use via 'talk'.

From merely telling his own drinking story at a group meeting, to twelfth stepping and sponsoring newcomers, the AA member is actively 'help-talking' fellow alcoholics. In learning to tell his story appropriately, for example, the newcomer is transforming his past experiences into something which can be used. His 'story' provides yet another story for the group to draw on and identify with. It is a means of distancing him from the 'unhappy' past experience and it is his 'personal example' to use in the intricate talk involved in Twelfth Stepping and sponsorship. It is a vehicle for carrying each member's own set of problems and, since problems change, so do members' stories. As time goes by, the talk moves away from the drinking experience to include items of the member's history *in* AA. The shift is from problems and alcohol to recovery and, most important, relationships.

Subsequent chapters will examine the crucial role of friendship within AA, with a view to showing how it sustains the AA member's world outside the group meeting and enables him to manage everyday living problems by taking the AA method outside the group. This chapter has shown that through AA talk, members changed from passive 'alcoholics' to 'recovering alcoholics'. By changing the way the alcoholic talks about himself and his place in the world AA enables him to talk himself out of his alcoholism. As one member reflected, 'I think in AA we become compulsive talkers. But at least it's a better compulsion than boozing'.

4 COPING THROUGH INVOLVEMENT

> Activity is common and necessary . . . The emphasis is
> upon 'doing' rather than upon intellectual pursuits or
> emotional, cathartic release. (Barish 1971)

Sharing the problem through identification and understanding is a crucial part of the self-help process of Alcoholics Anonymous. But it is not enough. For a drinker to 'recognise' that he is an alcoholic and that there are other people around him who are managing to handle their alcoholism is not sufficient to enable him to handle his own problem too.

As in other self-help groups, Alcoholics Anonymous members have to *do* as well as share; they have to act as well as empathise. In one of the best reviews of self-help activity Marie Killilea (1976) extracted seven core characteristics of self-help groups and their processes to which researchers have given particular emphasis. These she lists as:

1. *Common experience of members:* the belief that among the primary characteristics of self-help groups is the fact that the care giver has the same disability as the care receiver.

2. *Mutual help and support:* the fact that the individual is a member of a group that meets regularly in order to provide mutual aid.

3. *The helper principle:* which draws attention to the fact that in a situation in which people help others with a common problem it may be the helper who benefits most from the exchange.

4. *Differential association:* which emphasises the reinforcement of self-concepts of normality, which hasten the individual's separation from commitment to their previous deviant identities.

5. *Collective will-power and belief:* the tendency of each person to look to others in the group for validation of his feelings and attitudes.

6. *Importance of information:* the promotion of greater factual information of the problem condition as opposed to intrapsychic understanding.

7. *Constructive action toward shared goals:* the notion that self-help groups are action-oriented, their philosophy being that members learn by doing and are changed by doing.

Some of these features of self-help are more characteristic of groups other than Alcoholics Anonymous. The importance of information about the details of the condition, for example, is not important in AA, for the reasons discussed in the previous chapter; members are concerned with how to handle the problem not with how they came to get it. For some groups, whose problems are rather more specific and technical, the sharing of information about how members can cope with everyday practicalities and prevent a recurrence or accentuation of the problem is an important part of the self-help. In the U and I Club, for example, giving practical information constitutes almost the whole of the organisation's work. Most of the queries they get about vaginal infection are handled by recommending the founder's book (Kilmartin 1973) since U and I feel that this distillation of experiences covers everything the cystitis sufferer is likely to need; description of symptoms, some frequent causes, social and medical outcomes, medical treatments, self-help treatments and advice on prevention.

Coping with the Stigma

This sharing of practical information is one part of the deconstruction of the shared problem. Another facet of deconstruction is handling the stigma of the problem, because in addition to the practical difficulties of the condition there may be the social discredibility of being a person with the condition. An article in the magazine *Honey* (Brown 1976) under the heading 'Big Problems for Little People' highlights this distinction.

> The physical limitations of restricted growth are relatively easy to overcome — or at least learn to live with. Clothes can be made to measure and household appliances, and even cars, can be specially adapted to suit the little person's needs. Telephone kiosks, door handles and shaver points can, of course, present problems, but Mr Pocock carries a neat briefcase which opens into two steps for just such eventualities.

Clearly what makes such technical problems so difficult to live with is the way in which they are interpreted by the person himself or by other people: 'What is distressing for people of restricted growth is the way in which . . . people don't respect the fact that little people have an opinion, a view on life and that they want to contribute'.

Stigma is felt. As one of the leaflets of the Society for Skin Camouflage puts it 'anyone who has *felt different*, be it from class, colour, creed, accident, birth or disease, from the man whose balance

is impaired by losing three toes to the teenager whose romantic dreams
are blighted by acne , knows what it is like to be stigmatised'. Indeed,
the feeling of being stigmatised can be so intense as to dominate a
person's life. People describe themselves as feeling guilty, ashamed,
inadequate, having no place in life, nothing to contribute, worthless,
distressed, angry and finally alone, since in the end there may be a
gradual slide into secrecy, seclusion and isolation. Many alcoholics
described how, in the end, they knew that other people were discussing
them as totally worthless people who were unable to control their
drinking and thus their lives. Many women, in particular, hide away,
fearing to go out and face their neighbours and their friends who 'were
always on the look out for signs of drinking, and by that time, I
usually displayed them'. A familiar feature was to withdraw into a
lonely world, not only of self-pity but of self-disgust.

> I thought that they were right. And they were. It was awful to
> realise in my sane and sober moments that the people who
> shunned and despised me were absolutely right. I shunned and
> despised myself. Only I was stuck with me. You've no idea how it
> felt to be constantly doing the thing that made me hate myself.

People who become stigmatised, marked out and devalued by themselves and by others, need to regain their sense of personal worth. They
do not just need to find solutions to practical problems, they need to
change as people. And self-help groups enable people with problems to
do just that.

There is more to coping with stigma than getting together with
people who share the same problem and realising that you are not alone.
The mechanics for enhancing the member's self-esteem vary from group
to group. Some like the National Association for the Childless and
Childfree suggest that one should think positively about a lifestyle
without children rather than accepting an outsider's view that childless-
ness is a sign of failure or an indication of irresponsibility or selfishness.
Many other groups encourage their members to sort through their
feelings of inadequacy, anger, frustration and low self-esteem in group
discussion, while others offer counselling and others intimate support.

But as well as coming to accept one's situation without guilt, thinking
positively about oneself and enhancing one's self-esteem, self-help
groups can enable a person to turn defects, disabilities or shortcomings
into something of positive value. This was what Henrietta Seiberling
(1971) thought had been the real value of AA for Bill Wilson, one of

the two co-founders.

> Bill did a grand job. We can all see in his life what the Oxford group
> people had told us in their message: that if we turn our lives to God
> and let him run it, he will take our shortcomings and make them
> valuable in his way and give us our heart's desire. And when I got
> the word that Bill had gone on, I sat there, and it was just as if some-
> one had spoken to me again on top of my head. Something said to
> me, 'Verily, verily, he has received his reward'. So I went to the Bible,
> and there it was, in Matthew 6. Then I looked at Bill's story in
> *Alcoholics Anonymous* where Bill had said that all his failures were
> because he always wanted people to think he was somebody. In the
> first edition of the book, he said he always wanted to make his mark
> among people. And by letting God run his life, God took his ego and
> gave him his heart's desire in God's way. And when he was gone, he
> was on the front page of the *New York Times*, famous all over the
> world. So it does verify what the Oxford group people had told him.

The aim of any destigmatising effort is to enable members to get to
the stage of seeing themselves as being ordinary. Not only that but to be
seen by other people as ordinary as well. Peter Houghton, the founder
of the National Association of the Childless and Childfree wrote that 'the
childless are under the same pressure as the childfree and their common
interest lies in trying to make it *quite an unremarkable thing* not to
have any children'. The alcoholic, because of the way AA emphasises
the nature of alcoholism, can be absolved of the responsibility for
being an alcoholic: he is simply 'not as other men'. On the other hand,
he is fully responsible for remaining a sober alcoholic and so must
believe that not drinking is not only essential for him, but a reasonable
and acceptable thing for any person to do. Just as the non-smoker has
to be confident and willing enough to maintain his right to a smoke-
free environment so the alcoholic has to be confident enough to
establish his position as a non-drinker. In addition, he has to come to
realise that this does not make him less of a person, it does not mean
that he is unintelligent, or without a sense of humour, or untrustworthy,
or unbeautiful. It means, merely, that he will not be a consumer of
alcohol.

But coping with stigma entails more than just building up members'
self-esteem and persuading them that they are people of value, despite
their problem. It means that effort has to be put into persuading 'the

world out there as well'. People who do not have 'the problem' must be educated as well as those who do. They must be made to understand, rather than just react, if self-help groups are to be more than the mere closeting together of people who share not only a problem but a sense of failure, distress and persecution. Most self-help groups, therefore, aim to develop a sense of awareness of 'their problem' in the community at large. Most have pamphlets which explain the condition, which set out the difficulties faced by those with the problem and which often pinpoint the aims of the organisation in terms of fighting for a change, reorganisation or reallocation of services for people with the problem.

Much of the Alcoholics Anonymous literature is designed to explain the alcoholic to spouses, employers, friends, children and professions who are faced with having to do something for people who have some kind of alcohol-related problem.

TO HUSBANDS

If your wife seems to have a drinking problem, and has a sincere desire to do something about it, this booklet can be helpful to both of you. It can give *you* the facts about a relatively new approach to alcoholism that is helping thousands of men and women to live productive lives without alcohol. Once you understand this approach, you will be in a better position to help *your wife* face her problem realistically. If she is still drinking you may, for example, wish to discuss the Alcoholics Anonymous programme with her, pointing out that it is working successfully for many women whose experiences parallel hers.

This pamphlet *The Alcoholic Wife: A Message to Husbands* (1954) then goes on to discuss the importance of 'Facing the Problem', to give details about Alcoholics Anonymous and then to indicate 'How You Can Help'. In addition, there is literature explaining the relationship of AA to other helping organisations. One brief pamphlet is headed *If You Are A Professional: AA Wants to Work with You* (1972c) and explains:

Long before AA came into existence, in 1935, physicians, hospitals, churches, and other agencies and professional people provided life-saving aid to alcoholics, and they still do. We are profoundly grateful for the unselfish dedication of people like you to the welfare of people like us. . . Obviously it is not true that *only* an alcoholic can help an alcoholic. Our individual histories clearly show us that non-alcoholics do many things for alcoholics that AA does not do.

The pamphlet then goes on to list the many things that AA is not equipped to provide: detoxification; hospitalisation; medication; professional psychological, legal, mental, vocational and employment counselling; community organisation; law-enforcement; professional research; scientific training and education and much more. Then follows a description of the 'useful service' which AA offers. Another pamphlet stresses that the nature of AA's relationship with other organisations is *Cooperation but not Affiliation*.

While all this literature certainly serves to make people aware of Alcoholics Anonymous and undoubtedly helps many people to face and respond realistically to their own and other people's problems, it also plays an important part in the process of destigmatising the problem by changing the way in which the outside world sees the alcoholic and his alcoholism. By emphasising a simple disease model of alcoholism, AA have played a significant part in making it quite normal for most members of the general population, whether drinkers or not, to believe that the alcoholic is a sick rather than a morally weak person.

One way in which some self-help groups enhance members' self-esteem, while at the same time changing the attitudes of outsiders, is through integration. For some groups, meetings are opportunities not merely for people with the same problem to meet together, but for people with the problem to meet 'outsiders'. Breakthrough Trust, for example, aim to bring deaf and hearing people into as much contact as possible with each other and so alleviate much of the isolation, apathy and frustration that deafness imposes. By bringing members together on equal terms in the Trust 'they educate each other in the skills of communication and consequently a deeper understanding is gained'. Breakthrough Trust recognise, more clearly than many self-help groups, that those around the person with 'the problem' have a problem too. Not being able to communicate with a deaf person is a problem for the hearing person as much as for the deaf. It is not as dominating but, in many situations and relationships, it is just as disabling.

Alcoholics Anonymous do not have such a clear policy of integration, but certainly encourage and welcome people at their open meetings. Outsiders and other interested parties can certainly

learn something of what it is like to be an alcoholic from the many
stories and experiences which are presented. But the style of the routine
AA meeting makes it impossible for a non-alcoholic to be anything
more than an audience on the sidelines of the main performance. There
is no sense in which non-alcoholics are members together with
alcoholics.

Coping with stigma, the second strand of deconstructing the
alcoholic's problem, involves the realisation that one is not alone, that
there are others like you and that they understand and appreciate your
problems, ideas and aspirations. But coping with stigma involves self-
help groups in much more than the sharing of experiences and
identification. People as well as their problems have to be focused on
and people have to be changed. Members have to be encouraged to
relearn that they have a value, a contribution to make and a full place
to occupy in the world. They may not be drinkers any more, but both
they and outsiders have to recognise that neither this nor any of the
member's problems, whether they are personal or practical, invalidate
the alcoholic's membership of the human race.

Self-help groups like Alcoholics Anonymous are not merely forums
for *de*constructing members' problems by coping with practicalities and
by coping with stigma. Self-help is, in addition, a much more positive
process which enables members to *re*construct a new way of living
through project work. As Killilea pointed out 'Constructive action
toward shared goals' is a feature of much self-help group work. It
means that self-help groups like AA are action oriented,'their
philosophy being that members learn by doing and are changed by
doing'.

Involvement in Activities

One of the most widespread beliefs about Alcoholics Anonymous is
that membership of the fellowship involves little more than attending
formal weekly meetings. This idea is not unreasonable since as Leach
and associates (1969) have pointed out, the meeting is usually 'the
first and only distinguishable AA activity in which all the members of
a local group participate at the same time'. Nevertheless, as AA
members are well aware, being in AA involves far more than just going
to meetings. The 1976 survey of AA members in England and Wales
revealed that in addition to going to meetings and talking at meetings
members showed a high level of involvement in other activities both
inside and outside the meeting. It is clear, moreover, that these other
activities are not mere 'optional extras' but, for most members, an

integral part of the self-help process of Alcoholics Anonymous.

Earlier chapters showed that current AA members attended an average of just over two meetings a week. Moreover, it was not just newcomers with the injunction 'ninety meetings in ninety days' ringing in their ears who felt the need to go to more than a meeting a week, since sixty per cent of those who had been in AA for over ten years had been to more than one meeting a week in the past month. As well as attending meetings more often than is commonly imagined AA members tend to go to the meetings of more than one group. Seventy per cent of current members had attended the meetings of at least two different groups in the month prior to the survey while about one in three had been to more than three different groups.

In the previous chapter it was seen that over eighty per cent of current members had told their personal story at an AA meeting. Talking, in fact, was extremely important to members whether it was telling stories, taking part in discussions about particular issues in the AA programme of recovery or just briefly 'chatting' before and after the formal parts of the meeting. As one member put it: 'A lot gets done after the meeting. People have coffee and they sit and chat maybe for an hour until they get thrown out. Often a lot of goodies come out then. I often get more out of the chatting after-wards than the main part of the meeting'.

There is more to being an AA member for most people, however, than going to meetings, telling one's story and chatting. These are important activities, but are by no means the whole story. Among other activities are reading the AA literature, office holding, going to conventions and conferences, twelfth stepping and sponsorship and talking about AA to outside organisations.

In an important way the message of AA is carried by the literature and everyone comes across some kind of AA literature very soon in their membership. Available to the member are twenty-three pamphlets on the AA programme of recovery ranging from P.1 *This is AA* via *Is AA For You?*, *How it Works* and *Questions and Answers on Sponsorship* to P.23 *AA and the Armed Forces.* There are nine further pamphlets on aspects of AA unity and service dealing with the organisation and traditions of the fellowship. These deal with such topics as *The Co-Founder of AA, AA Tradition – How it Developed* and *Understanding Anonymity*. Five pamphlets are specifically for professional and business people who might want to know about AA in the course of their work, while twelve further pamphlets deal with the relationship between AA and the general public. Apart from directories,

wallet cards and parchments on which particular items such as the
twelve steps are reproduced, and special items like cards for doctors'
surgeries there are the five AA books.

Alcoholics Anonymous (1939) is the 'basic book' and contains an
account of how AA works, with chapters on working with others and
messages to wives and employers. The major part of the book is, however, given over to the personal stories of the early members and upon
which the programme of recovery is based.

> We, of Alcoholics Anonymous, are more than one hundred men and
> women who have recovered from a seemingly hopeless state of mind
> and body. To show other alcoholics *precisely how we have recovered*
> is the main purpose of this book. For them, we hope these pages
> will prove so convincing that no further authentication will be
> necessary. We think this account of our experiences will help any-
> one to better understand the alcoholic. (From the foreword to the
> first edition.)

Alcoholics Anonymous Comes of Age (1957) is AA's own history.
The first part of the book presents 'a panoramic sketch' of the St Louis
Convention in 1955 at which 'the fellowship of Alcoholics Anonymous
came of age and assumed full responsibility for all its affairs'. At this
meeting the General Service Conference of AA took over from the old
timers and founders 'custody of AA's Twelve Traditions and the
guardianship of its world services'. The second part of the book contains three edited lectures by Bill W. on Recovery, Unity and Service,
while in the third part there are the addresses given at the St Louis
convention by various friends of AA in which they spoke of their
association with AA and their part in its development. Here again AA
is demonstrating the importance, which it recognised right at the
beginning, of gaining the approval of, and working closely with, other
people who have some part to play in the handling of alcohol-related
problems. This, as far as AA is concerned is not just good sense or
good manners, but an essential part of making the fellowship a credible
and understandable organisation which can take disabled and discredited
people and deconstruct their problems and reconstruct their lives.

Twelve Steps and Twelve Traditions (1952b) contains an exposition
of the development and meaning of these key principles. *The AA Way
of Life* (1967) is a collection of excerpts from the writings of Bill W.,
which deal with 332 facets of the programme of recovery from
'personality change' and 'seeking guidance' to 'coping with anger' and

'time versus money'. Both these books supply texts for 'discussion' and 'closed' meetings where members attempt to identify the meaning for themselves of particular aspects of AA principles and practice.

The final book *Came to Believe* (1973) contains members' contributions dealing specifically with AA as 'a spiritual programme'.

> *Came to Believe* is designed as an outlet for the rich diversity of convictions implied in 'God as we understood Him'. Most of the material was written expressly for this booklet, in response to an appeal issued by the General Service Office.

In addition to these books and pamphlets are the AA magazine, *Share*, and *Box 514*. *Share* is the United Kingdom equivalent of the American magazine, *Grapevine*. It is produced 'by AA members who work in the fields of publishing and journalism and who are prepared to bring their professional skills to the service of the fellowship' (*Annual Report* 1977). *Share* comes out monthly and contains contributions by members. *Box 514* is a quarterly newsletter from the General Service Office in London giving news of events and development in the fellowship.

Members were asked in the survey about whether they had read certain of the AA publications. Women tended to be more regular readers than men. However, irrespective of their sex and length of time in AA, ten per cent of current members had never read the 'Big Book', (*Alcoholics Anonymous* 1939) and a further thirteen per cent had only read it very rarely. As can be seen from Table 4.1 other kinds of literature were much more popular. *Share* was the favourite with two thirds of all current members reading it regularly. On the other hand *Box 514*, the newsletter, was much less popular. Half of the current members of AA had never read it at all. Several copies of *Box 514* are sent direct to the secretary of each group and the intention is that the

Table 4.1: Reading AA Literature

Literature	Regularly %	Occasionally %	Rarely %	Never %	Total N
Share	66.3	20.7	7.7	5.3	169
Pamphlets	64.7	30.0	5.3	0.0	170
'Big Book'	35.9	40.0	13.5	10.6	170
Box 514	16.1	13.7	20.2	50.0	168

secretary shall circulate copies so that each member can keep up with latest developments.

Although reading the literature is important, it is not in itself enough to ensure that AA members recover from their alcohol-related problems. As one member said, he certainly 'could not have existed on the literature alone. It was the pure understanding of the people I was with, the companionship, compassion and being with other people. I could not have just picked it up from the literature'. One way of getting greater involvement with other AA members is through office holding.

At every AA meeting there will be some members with particular responsibilities. In addition to the usual officers, chairman, secretary and treasurer, there are a number of members who might be called on to speak or who may volunteer to make tea, put out chairs or help collect the contributions. Table 4.2 shows that involvement in these activities is related to a member's sex and length of time in the fellowship. Overall, the proportion of the membership who have held office is very high compared with other kinds of organisations, since each office is held only for a short fixed period and then relinquished to someone else. In this way the chances of holding office increase steadily with length of time in the fellowship. Women tend to be slightly less likely to hold office than men.

Table 4.2: Office Holding

Office Held	Under 1 %	1 < 2 %	Years in AA 2 < 4 %	4 < 6 %	6 < 10 %	10 and Over %	Men %	Women %	N	Total %
Secretary	11.4	26.9	53.6	60.9	55.6	70.0	51.9	33.9	76	45.0
Contact person	13.9	32.0	35.7	60.9	42.3	54.8	43.4	30.6	65	38.5
Treasurer	8.3	38.5	39.3	60.9	40.7	54.8	41.7	33.9	66	38.6
Manned switchboard	2.8	19.2	21.4	21.7	16.7	26.7	15.7	21.0	30	17.5

The importance of office holding to some individual members should not be underestimated. One AA member explained what being a secretary meant to him. 'It's kept me involved. I find that if I'm not involved at one meeting of my home group, I tend to wander. . . It was good for me to speak as well as to sit up the front. I couldn't just hide in the background'.

Opportunities for involvement in the fellowship of Alcoholics Anonymous exist outside regular AA meetings. There are a group of events which form a different sort of meeting. These may be concerned with official AA business such as AA's conference, intergroup meetings, the annual convention, and mini-conventions or social events such as local dinner dances.

In Table 4.3, we can see that the high level of involvement is further reflected in the proportions of members who have attended AA's various formal functions. Members are less likely to have gone to intergroup meetings, which are a kind of regional AA meeting, and conference at which official AA business is discussed, than to an AA convention. This is because members are elected to the former position and longstanding members may feel newcomers are not sufficiently experienced in AA to represent their group. Nevertheless, it is perhaps surprising that as many as one in six 'newcomers', who have been in AA less than one year, have attended intergroup meetings. Also noteworthy is the fact that women are more likely than men to go to conventions but less likely to be representatives at the intergroup and conference meetings. This is consistent with the pattern of office holding noted above.

Table 4.3: Attending AA Events outside the Group

			Years in AA							
Events attended	Under 1 %	1 < 2 %	2 < 4 %	4 < 6 %	6 < 10 %	10 and Over %	Men %	Women %	N	Total %
Convention or mini-convention	30.6	50.0	67.9	78.3	74.1	80.0	56.1	71.0	104	61.5
Intergroup meeting	16.7	30.8	53.6	56.5	55.6	63.3	49.5	35.5	75	44.4
Conference	2.8	7.1	3.6	26.1	22.2	30.0	17.8	8.1	24	14.2

'Twelfth Stepping' and 'Sponsorship' are other important ways in which a member can become involved. These are significant in that they not only take the member outside the meeting, but also present an opportunity to 'carry the AA message'. Among outsiders, there is often some confusion surrounding the activities of twelfth stepping and sponsorship. The last of the 'Twelve Steps' states that, 'Having had a spiritual awakening as the result of these steps, we tried to carry this message to alcoholics and to practice these principles in all our affairs'. From Table 4.4, we can see that three-quarters of all current members have twelfth stepped a newcomer and also that by the time members have been in the fellowship for two years almost eighty per cent have twelfth stepped someone.

Table 4.4: Involvement in Twelfth Stepping

Ever twelfth stepped someone	Under 1 1 %	Years in AA 2 < 2 %	2< 4 %	4< 6 %	6< 10 %	10 and Over %	Men %	Women %	N	Total %
Yes	35.3	53.8	78.6	87.0	85.2	96.8	73.1	75.4	125	74.0
No	64.7	46.2	21.4	13.0	14.8	3.2	26.9	24.6	49	26.0

Most observers agree that twelfth stepping is crucially important for an AA member. It presents the opportunity for him to put his devalued and worthless past to good use, by drawing on his drinking history to help suffering alcoholics. For Bean (1975) 'This idea, that a person's experience is of value, is gratifying to anyone and is particularly heady stuff to the chronically self-depreciating alcoholic'. Indeed, she goes as far as to say that taking the twelfth step is seen by many as a 'guarantee of recovery'.

Twelfth stepping, however, is only an initial contact. Beyond that is the sponsorship system. The idea of sponsorship goes back to the early days of AA. As newcomers were attracted to the programme, a member with some period of sobriety became the new arrival's sponsor. The sponsor told of his own experience, explained the programme as he saw it, tried to help the newcomer over the rough spots by answering questions, encouraging him to get to AA meetings and meet other members.

Sponsorship, then, is twelfth step work, but with a continuing responsibility. It helps the newcomer by assuring him that there is at least one person who understands his problem fully, to whom he can turn without embarrassment when doubts, questions or difficulties linked to his problem arise. Sponsorship provides support and understanding when it is most needed. 'A sponsor' says AA (1958) 'does everything he can, within the limits of his experience and knowledge to help a newcomer get sober, and stay sober with the help of the AA program'. The pamphlet *Questions and Answers on Sponsorship* (1958) lists the following aspects of being a sponsor.

He shows by his own example and drinking history what AA has meant to him.

He encourages and helps the newcomer to attend a variety of AA meetings — to get a number of viewpoints and interpretations of the AA program.

If the newcomer isn't at first sure whether or not he is an alcoholic, the sponsor encourages him to keep an open mind on AA.

He introduces the newcomer to other members, particularly to those who may share the new man's job or social interests.

A male sponsor works largely with men alcoholics, while the woman alcoholic finds she works best with her own sex.

He makes himself available to the newcomer when the latter feels he has special problems.

He goes over the meaning of the Twelve Steps, and emphasises their importance.

He urges the newcomer to join in group activities as soon as he is ready.

He impresses on the newcomer the meaning of the Anonymity Tradition and the importance of all the Traditions.

He explains the program to relatives of the alcoholic, if this appears to be useful — showing them how they can help in the new man's recovery.

Finally, he encourages the newcomer to work with other alcoholics as soon as he is fit and ready to do so.

Although the sponsor is clearly an important support for many newcomers the sponsor is urged to underscore the fact 'that it is the recovery program — not the sponsor's personality or position — that is important'. The newcomer is taught to lean on the program, not on the sponsor.

In spite of the long list of things which the sponsor might do, AA is careful not to tell him *how* to do it. Each member is free 'to approach sponsorship as his own experience and personality may suggest'. This means, of course, that there are many styles of sponsorship, theoretically geared to the needs of the newcomer, but usually based on the beliefs of the sponsor about what being a sponsor entails. While AA warns of the danger of being too firm, of being too over protective, and of being too casual the final decision on 'the right approach' rests with the sponsor and to a lesser extent the group and, only occasionally, on the newcomer, if he is aware of his needs and articulate and willing enough to express them.

Sponsorship, like twelfth stepping, is valuable not only to the person being sponsored but also the person who does the sponsoring. One member explained how he felt when he was asked to be a sponsor. 'One night he asked me to be his sponsor. I thought, "Bloody hell". It seemed like the final accolade at the time. I thought, "Things have moved. I've got a lot better". I'm not boosting myself because I'm his sponsor but it's nice to see the programme working on someone else and it all seemed very worthwhile.' Sponsorship strengthens the experienced member's sobriety. 'In some mysterious manner', says AA (1958), 'the act of sharing seems to make it easier for a member to live without alcohol. By helping others, alcoholics find that they can help themselves'. In other words alcoholics stay sober by being involved.

Just over half the current members had been a sponsor at some time, and, on average, members had sponsored three people. Table 4.5 shows that sponsoring is significantly related to the length of time a person has been in the fellowship, with two years being an important landmark. Those who have been in the fellowship for over two years are over four times as likely to have sponsored someone than those who have been in AA for less than two years.

Table 4.5: Involvement in Sponsorship

Ever been a sponsor	Under 1 %	1 < 2 %	2 < 4 %	4 < 6 %	6 < 10 %	10 and Over %	Men %	Women %	N	Total %
Yes	16.7	15.4	60.7	78.3	59.3	87.1	52.8	50.0	88	51.8
No	83.3	84.6	39.3	21.7	40.7	12.9	47.2	50.0	82	48.2

Ninety per cent of members who became sponsors did so within three years of attending their first meeting and eighty per cent of those who have acted as sponsors to other members are still in touch with the person they first sponsored. It is also interesting that, on average, over one in four of those members who have been in the fellowship for six years or more have *never* been a sponsor, which suggests that sponsoring someone, though desirable, is not essential for continued

AA membership.

There are at least two major benefits for a member who is involved in twelfth stepping and sponsorship. The first is that these activities change the member's focus of attention from himself and his problems, to other people's problems. When a sponsor calls on his sponsee to go to a meeting, the newcomer may feel overwhelmed with his concern, but as the sponsor may point out, he is doing it as much for himself as for the newcomer. As one member told us, 'While I'm thinking about someone else, I'm not thinking about me and all my problems. And if someone wants to go (to a meeting) I will go or even put the idea into their heads, but it's for me'. It is in this sense that AA says theirs is a 'selfish' programme.

The second benefit of twelfth stepping and sponsorship is that these activities provide new non-drinking experiences. As active involvement in AA continues, and as members gradually move away from their experience of problem drinking, their 'new' everyday life is added to by stages in AA life and aspects of life outside AA which can be cited in contrast to their past, but ever remembered, problem drinking.

Unlike twelfth stepping and sponsorship, talking about AA to outside organisations is obviously something which requires the member to leave the comfort of the group environment and place himself in a minority among non-AAs. Table 4.6 shows that just over one third of all current members had done this and it is worth considering that of those members who had done so, sixty per cent of them had been in the fellowship for more than four years. As one member, who had spoken to schools, prison groups and Eighteen Plus groups put it, 'It was good to realise that there are groups around who are interested enough to call on us to talk, but was great to realise that I could actually go and do it'.

Table 4.6: Talking to Outside Organisations about AA

Ever talked to outside organisation	Under 1 %	1 < 2 %	Years in AA 2 < 4 %	4 < 6 %	6 < 10 %	10 and over %	Men %	Women %	N	Total %
Yes	11.1	11.5	25.0	34.8	55.6	71.0	36.1	32.3	59	34.7
No	88.9	88.5	75.0	65.2	44.4	29.0	63.9	67.7	111	65.3

Coping through Involvement

In self-help groups problems are not just shared, although this is a vital first step, they are coped with. Coping, however, means coping with the person who *has* the problem not just with the technicalities and practicalities *of* the problem. Coping with stigma entails continuous support and a re-education campaign directed at both the member and the outside world. Members are encouraged to recognise that there is a full place in life for people with their problem. The outside world has to be told that those with the problem need not only help and support but also as much opportunity as anyone else to make their own particular contribution to the way in which the world works.

Alcoholics Anonymous, like other self-help groups, is more than sharing and evangelising. It provides a forum for members to learn new skills and discover that by controlling their problem they can control their life. By being involved in AA activities, members build up a stock of experiences and expertise which enables them to handle not only their drinking problem but also everyday problems of living as well. By being part of a group which provides continuous mutual support in a variety of ways at a variety of times, members have the opportunity to be continuously involved in help-talking fellow sufferers. By being continuously involved members are able to cope with their problems and, thus, with themselves.

Although there are many long-standing members of Alcoholics Anonymous who have never held office, never sponsored a newcomer and never even told their story, they are a very small minority of the whole fellowship. They demonstrate that full involvement is not essential but, on the other hand, it is clear that the way AA enables most people to handle their problem is through involvement. Not only that but those people who are less involved in the fellowship are more likely to have dropped out at some time in the past. Table 4.7 shows, for example, that those who have been in the fellowship for over six years and have never sponsored anyone else are much more likely to have dropped out at some time in the past than those who have sponsored someone.

Similar associations between dropping out and non-involvement were found in respect of reading the 'Big Book', Twelfth Stepping a newcomer, reading *Box 514* and being a group secretary.

As time goes by the focus of the member's concern gradually changes from his own problem and maintaining his own sobriety, to helping others to maintain theirs. The member's own sobriety is still the main concern, but the method of maintaining it changes from

Table 4.7: Sponsorship and Dropping Out by Members with over 6 Years in AA

| Ever sponsored someone | Number of times they have dropped out | | | | Total |
	Never %	Once %	More than Once %	N	%
Yes	51.2	20.9	27.9	43	74.1
No	20.0	13.3	66.7	15	25.9

receiving support, help and encouragement and identifying with others who have succeeded, to giving support to others, being identified with and depended upon and accepting responsibility through involvement in the formal offices and activities of the fellowship. Long-standing members are involved in carrying the AA message not merely to newcomers but to the world outside AA; to other organisations. Sobriety is achieved in AA not merely by *not* doing something – not drinking – but by doing something – being continuously involved.

Eventually, the important test of the AA member's sobriety comes when he is neither attending AA meetings nor doing formal AA work. Those who are unaware of what AA does might accept that the fellowship works while members are attending formal meetings and, in that respect, it might seem no different from other methods of handling alcohol-related problems. The crucial difference, however, is that for many alcoholics, AA also carries on working when the AA member has left the meeting for home and helps maintain his sobriety until the next meeting. Members are quite aware that this is the different period. As one member explained, 'This is it. Trying to get through the time when the pubs were open. When they shut, well, that's all right'. The way AA helps during the danger time is by taking the group beyond the meeting into the everyday life of the member. AA for some people becomes a 'way of life'.

AA AS A WAY OF LIFE

> AA has not given me a cure — there's no cure for us 'alkies' — it
> has given me a new way of life. ('E.R.' in Ritchie 1948)

The great majority of the health problems which people face are short-
lived. Either they go away of their own accord or respond to some kind
of self-treatment or medical intervention. They do not cause any great
threat to or upset in the routine of the sufferer's everyday life. They
are, in fact, a part of 'normal' life. Other problems, however, are much
more difficult to tidy away. They are major or life disrupting because
they represent a threat to *someone's* everyday world. And self-help
groups, because they operate in several crucially different ways from
conventional help, often deal with these major problems which cannot
be handled in the normal way. Those who manage to successfully get
involved in a self-help group accomplish a reorientation in relation to
the way in which problems are usually handled. They move from a conception of problem solving where life is experienced *in spite of* problems
which are got rid of as swiftly as possible, to one where life is
experienced *through* problems, which are continuously taken note of
and in some cases are a source of pride or even enjoyed.

Learning to live through problems and incorporating problem
solving into the routine of one's everyday life is learnt in the self-help
group. Through becoming involved in Alcoholics Anonymous, for
example, members learn to accept the problem as part of them, 'the
alcoholic', and learn to live a life in which the fact of being an
alcoholic will always be a part. Being an alcoholic the AA way becomes
a way of life. And this new way of life is constructed in the group.

From Activities to Friendships

Being an AA member does not just mean being involved in formal AA
activities. It is a matter of forming relationships and friendships with
other AA members which in turn leads to informal activity outside AA
meetings. Table 5.1 shows that three quarters of the members in the
survey said that they had made a lot of new friends in AA and this was
even true of over sixty per cent of members who had been in the
fellowship for less than a year. But as can be seen from Table 5.2, this
was not just a case of making additional friends, since only thirty per
cent of members still saw most of the friends they had before they

Table 5.1: New Friends made in AA

Have you made new friends in AA?	Under 1	1 < 2	Years in AA 2 < 4	4 < 6	6 < 10	10 and over	Men	Wo-men	Total	
	%	%	%	%	%	%	%	%	N	%
Yes, a lot	61.1	61.6	89.3	82.6	80.8	83.9	76.6	74.2	128	75.7
Yes, a few	36.1	34.6	10.7	17.4	19.2	16.1	21.5	25.8	39	23.1
No	2.8	3.0	0.0	0.0	0.0	0.0	1.9	0.0	2	1.2

Table 5.2: Proportion of Old Non-AA Friends still seen

Do you still see old non-AA friends?	Under 1	1 < 2	Years in AA 2 < 4	4 < 6	6 < 10	10 and over	Men	Wo-men	Total	
	%	%	%	%	%	%	%	%	N	%
Most of them	41.7	38.5	28.6	43.5	15.4	16.1	28.0	35.5	52	30.8
Some of them	27.8	34.6	39.3	26.1	34.6	54.8	40.2	29.0	61	36.1
Hardly any of them	16.7	19.2	25.0	4.3	34.6	12.9	15.0	25.8	32	18.9
None of them	13.8	7.7	7.1	26.1	15.4	16.2	16.8	9.7	24	14.2

first came to AA.

Even among those who had been in AA for less than a year, the majority had separated themselves from some of their old friends. This is a familiar pattern in self-help groups and is part of the process of separating off from past experiences and starting to build a new set of relationships and a new way of life. Some members were quite clear about what it was that their old friends were unable to provide for them which they then found in AA. Peter explained:

In the past, my friends used to show me concern about my drinking and give all kinds of weird and wonderful advice, but they were often drunk at the time themselves. In AA the people I know and care about care about me too. That means they don't just talk off the top of their heads, but they demonstrate their concern. They follow up their comments and see if it's working. They follow through, that's it. That's the big thing in AA — there is always a feeling that people are really interested in being sure you've got over the difficult bit. They don't just say the first thing that comes into their head and then forget.

Harrison Trice (1958) was one of the first people outside AA to recognise that time spent with AA members in leisure was an important factor in maintaining the member's sobriety. He pointed out that, 'individual members get together to eat lunch, drink coffee. They meet after work, to bowl, fish and play cards. These informal contacts extend the relationship developed in formal meetings'. For some people these informal contacts mean getting together with some-one before the meeting.

> I went over there to speak. I met this bloke and we went and had cups of tea and I had chocolate eclairs, as I will. This was before the meeting. There's a little tea shop near the station. I always go in there and have pots of tea. The meeting didn't start till quarter to eight and I was there at seven so we had plenty of time for cups of tea and then on to the meeting.

It might be a discussion immediately after the meeting:

> A lot gets done after the meeting. A lot of talking gets done once the meeting's over. People have coffee and they sit and chat maybe for an hour until you get thrown out. And often a lot of the goodies come out then. It's like last orders. The lights go off. 'Everybody out!' The last part can often be better.

Or members might reassemble at someone's house after a meeting.

> Sometimes, they'll say, 'Well, what are you doing now?' 'Oh going home'. 'How about coffee?' Off we zoom to some bugger's house. It could be anywhere. And eventually after thinking it would be an early night, half ten, it could be a bloody midnight, two o'clock touch. . . We just sit and what with coffee and you'll find some people will talk a lot easier in their own surroundings or in friendly surroundings than a bare room with chairs around a table. I had a few back here in the summer. On Sunday they were doing similar. Somebody phoned up and she said, 'Are you coming?' This is the sort of thing where you just sit and chat about anything and it's not

a true meeting.

For some people the most useful and valuable contacts were those which were totally unconnected with the meeting. These contacts were embedded into the rest of the member's life where the possibility of trouble always lurks. 'It's easy at the meetings, but when you really appreciate that the others care is when it's away from meetings and really in your life'. It might be a brief meeting at work:

> I think I'm quite fortunate in working with other people, AA people. They're working in other parts of the company. They'll look in and say 'How are you?' I maybe will ring up and say, 'Look, so and so's not feeling too good. If you're down that way look in on him'. Sometimes I wander in and see him and come back after listening to him and he'll listen to me. Sometimes it can be just general chatting not booze. It can be any old chat.

or a brief telephone call:

> I phone in tea-breaks. Just a two minute call, really, that's all it needs. I realize that just to make a little call is so good. I used to get called in my early days. It's just the thought that somebody suddenly thought, 'I wonder how Steve's doing?' And they just pick up the phone and it can make you feel good.

A delicate balance has to be struck, however, between friendships in the context of AA and friendship in which the AA dimension is missing. Philip described how one relationship which began in AA did not retain the vital AA ingredient:

> He said at one point 'We get on well, we'll just be mates'. I said, 'fine' but eventually it got to be more mates than it was AA. It got just being ordinary mates and nothing else. I've found that the main reasons aren't main any more for him. The reasons he started coming to AA seem to have changed. Life has taken over and AA is just a sideline.

It may be that his friend had 'grown out' of AA and felt able to manage without any discussion of the AA programme or any acknowledgement that AA was one of the dimensions of their relationship. This may have been all right for him, but Philip was not ready for this complete break

with the programme. He still wanted an 'AA friendship' with all that
this implied.

> When I came off the booze I entirely got rid of all the people who
> knew me when I was drinking. I faded people out and made new
> friends that knew me for what I am. I still see non-AAs of course. I
> had some friends down last week and we met for a meal. I knock
> about with this girl up the road. These aren't AA members. But
> I've found the danger for me at the moment is when my social life
> other than AA takes over from AA.

However, the social life and relationships based on AA which some
members found so valuable could be a barrier to others. AA was unhelpful for one member because:

> There were certain people who were very friendly and I was an out-
> sider. This might be imagination. This is my idea. I was an outsider
> of this little group who were sitting tight and going to AA regular.
> They seemed to cling together more. It was like a clique. I think
> that's what put me off . . . I found that it was just a sort of social
> club for these people. Just the clique. It might be good for some
> people, good luck to them. I'm not running AA down. I'm just
> saying that AA doesn't do anything for me.

AA members see each other outside the meeting, at each other's
homes, at work and on social occasions and these relationships are very
important. They carry the group's programme beyond the meeting into
the everyday life of the member. Table 5.3 shows that only seventeen
per cent of current members have never had another AA member as a

Table 5.3: Having another AA Member to your Home

Regularity of having other AAs to your home	Under 1 %	1 < 2 %	Years in AA 2 < 4 %	4 < 6 %	6 < 10 %	10 and over %	Men %	Women %	N	Total %
Regularly	16.7	23.1	25.0	34.8	48.0	51.6	34.3	29.1	55	32.4
Occasionally	30.6	42.3	53.6	52.2	40.0	32.2	33.3	41.9	62	36.5
Rarely	13.8	7.7	7.1	8.7	12.0	9.7	13.0	14.5	23	13.5
Never	38.9	26.9	14.3	4.3	0.0	6.5	19.4	14.5	30	17.6

guest in their homes. We can also see that almost half of those who had been in AA for less than one year saw other members in their homes at least 'occasionally'. Almost half of those who had been in AA over six years had AAs to their homes 'regularly'.

As well as seeing other AA members at their homes, almost forty per cent of members saw each other socially on other social occasions. The most frequently mentioned were when AAs went out together for meals, to cafes, discos and, surprisingly perhaps, to pubs, bars and cocktail parties. Members also went to sports events, met for rather more relaxed pastimes such as music, chess and bridge and accompanied each other to films, plays, concerts and on outings and holidays. Twenty per cent of members felt that such social meetings between AA members were an 'essential' part of the AA programme and a further fifty-five per cent recognised that they were a 'useful' part of the programme.

This informal socialising between AA members could be interpreted as an incidental sideline to the real work of formal AA activities. In a sense it is, since the informal activities grew out of the formal activities which are routinely shared among as large a proportion of members as possible. But it is much more than just an accidental accretion, it is an integral part of the self-help process. It is a way of ensuring that the perspective on alcoholism which is gained in the meeting is maintained outside the group.

Formal activities in the group enable people to turn their discredited past into something of use to other alcoholics. They enable members to look beyond their immediate problem and begin to think of other people and how they can help fellow members to find and maintain sobriety. But by acting as a focal point they bring people together to form relationships which begin the process of transferring the person with the problem from the confines of the group to the world outside. As such, these informal social activities between members who are friends are not just fortunate, or relevant, but a core part of the ultimate aim of all self-help groups like Alcoholics Anonymous namely, to enable members to build a new way of life.

Clearly friendships can develop in a wide variety of ways. Some self-help groups have specific social activities thereby signalling their belief that being in a group is more than handling the technicalities of the problem, while Alcoholics Anonymous, and some other groups, have their sponsorship systems which increase the likelihood of friendships though these 'arranged' relationships. But in whatever way friendships develop they are important.

The informal network of friendships and social contacts within AA like the other forms of involvement, is related to whether or not a person stays in or drops out of the fellowship. However, this is a complex relationship since for some long-standing members, who have exceeded the 5.3 average years of membership, an increase in informal activities with other AA members is associated with a progressive decline in regular attendance at formal meetings. When this happens, it might reflect a *growing* out of, rather than a *dropping* out of, the fellowship. Indeed such a maturing process seems to be the ultimate way that AA 'cures' alcoholism.

Time, Continuity and the AA Method

Underpinning the involvement, or project, approach to problem solving in self-help groups is the emphasis on time. Projects in many groups are specifically time-related such as the Gamblers Anonymous Pin Night to celebrate periods of time in the group, or the Weight Watchers' emphasis on goal weight, the weight to be achieved in a particular period of time.

But as well as working toward time targets there is the problem of time-filling. Powell (1975) has observed that when a person dis-associates from his earlier life pattern 'an inevitable hiatus is experienced'. 'Unstructured time is copiously available', he says, and large amounts of it can often be occasions for relapse, because there is nothing else to do so familiar patterns re-emerge.

For Alcoholics Anonymous, a group with one of the most explicit time-emphasising project approaches, the simple aim of the programme is easy to understand — never to drink again. But in order to develop a sober life a programme is needed which enables the alcoholic to manage the time between now and death. 'This is it', said Steve, 'trying to get through time'.

The most explicit scheduling of time is embodied in the twelve steps, from Step One in which there is the recognition of time past when drinking made life unmanageable through to Step Twelve when there is an acceptance of the role of AA in the future 'in all our affairs'. But although the steps are an important feature of the programme, they might not be rigidly followed: 'I'm not very good with the steps. I can't even remember them all. I know I did have a go. That's not the most important thing for me'. In any case, say AA (1961), the twelve steps, while at the heart of the AA programme are *suggestions* only: 'They are simply a statement of the personal experience of the first men and women who achieved sobriety in AA, in the days before the movement

even had a name. These steps worked for these people... They can
work for you'.

Failure to follow the steps themselves does not mean that the
formula of organising time and experience into past, present and
future is ignored. Indeed, explicit distinctions are often made between
time now and time past, between the member and his life now and in
the past, while references to origins and the 'first time' are frequently
made, particularly in the story of AA itself (*Alcoholics Anonymous
Comes of Age* 1957) where great attention is given to landmarks on the
movement's growth and development:

> About that time there appeared on the New York scene another
> character Fitz M., one of the most lovable people that AA will ever
> know... Fitz fell at once into hot argument with Henry about the
> religious content of the coming volume [*Alcoholics Anonymous*]...
> Out of this debate came the spiritual form and substance of the
> document, notably the expression 'God as we understood Him',
> which proved to be a ten-strike.

In the member's personal story the emphasis is on telling 'what you
were like, what happened when you came to AA and what you *are* like
now' (*Alcoholics Anonymous* 1939). This retrospective ordering of
events is not just a feature of twelfth-step work when one story is
presented for a newcomer to identify with. It is a feature of all stories,
which themselves change over time as different features or periods of
time are emphasised. Past experience is given meaning in relation to the
present. Time prior to the 'decision' to stop drinking is contrasted with
time afterwards. Time before AA is contrasted with time in AA. For a
newcomer the contrast may be the present with a confused past, while
as time in AA progresses a member can incorporate and re-evaluate
his early AA experiences. One member explained:

> In the early days, even though I was going to meetings I was still
> getting the same sort of feelings. But I didn't know this so I went to
> meetings and thought marvellous it's working. But I know now that
> without coming off the pills it just couldn't work. I don't think
> anything worked until the pills went. So I lost eighteen months of
> AA because I wasn't in my right mind. I know that now. Then I
> stopped going for a while. When I went back to AA I looked at it
> in a completely different light. They were talking about parts of
> the programme and I thought, 'What's this?' I didn't hear it before

but they must have mentioned it.

Or as Peter put it: 'I used to talk about all the escapades I got up to and Ken and one or two others said, "Your story will change". As time went on it did change. I remembered more. It didn't exactly change I suppose I saw it differently'.

As 'AA time' takes over, becoming itself recent experience, then for particular audiences the drinking experience may be only briefly mentioned or even not mentioned at all:

I went over to another group on Saturday. I did mainly recovery. I said, 'I'm not gonna do my drinking story. I've done it and I've done it'. One or two nodded in a knowledgeable way knowing that they'd done the same and they were thinking 'Thank God'. It can get much too easy. So we didn't do that and I spoke on recovery. First we read it in the book. We read how it works. I then spoke basing it on that – how it worked for me.

While time past is reconstructed and aspects of it related to the present, time in the present is narrowed down, and focused on. Time present is all important, time in the future is devalued:

For example, we take no pledges; we don't say that we will abstain from alcohol 'forever'. Instead we try what we call the 'Twenty-Four Hour Plan'. We concentrate on keeping sober for just the current twenty-four hours. . . If we feel the urge for a drink, we neither yield nor resist. We merely defer taking that particular drink until *tomorrow*. (AA 1957)

It is not only drinking which is dealt with in the twenty-four hour plan; there is a tendency for all long term planning to be, if not devalued, felt to be dangerous or too much to handle. Steve gave one example when:

A year or so back I wanted to buy a house. . . They got me to take out great insurance. They started on about pensions and when I was sixty-five and I thought, 'My God'. This is the thing trying to keep it simple, twenty-four hours at a time. They were leaping ahead in years, in decades. I thought, 'Bloody Hell'. For me I was a bit out of my depth.

Just as AA members may shun mortgages so the General Service

Office in London does not own its own building. As the General
Secretary put it:

> We don't own property, we wouldn't own property because this
> brings problems. We buy a lease and rent. On this property which
> has twelve years to go on the lease, who can tell in twelve years time,
> if this building is big enough in the first place, and we would want
> to remain here, and if so, what the lease is going to cost us. So let's
> not bother about what is going to happen in twelve years. Let's
> just do our best today, and the few spare pennies we have left
> guard them well.

But not everyone, of course, is willing to devalue their future. This
was one of the things which Kate felt was so bad about AA: 'All they
said was "If you can say to yourself just for today. Tomorrow I don't
know what I'm going to do". Well I don't believe in it you see. I
believe in long term things'.

Since particular problems may be there for *all time*, and since
relapses or 'slips' can happen *any time*, commitment to AA must be
full time. The newcomer, for example, is the 'life blood' not just
because of the opportunity he provides for members to do their
twelfth-step work, but because he illustrates how important it is to
keep such 'work' up. The newcomer or the slipped member demon-
strates the precariousness of the member's position and reminds him
of how he was in the past, as opposed to how he is now, and of how he
could be again in the future:

> I see some that have missed meetings and they drift off and
> eventually they drink and I think I'm glad I'm not doing any of
> those things. You might get someone say with seventeen years
> sobriety, one of the original ones who saw me in the early days,
> who's drinking again pretty bad. It's those sort of things that keep
> me on my toes. I can go out and have a drink, but by seeing them I
> know what happens. It's a gradual going down, the job gone, the
> wives and husbands have left. It's those sort of things that keeps me
> on my toes. I'm reminded of what I was like.

In addition to separating activity into manageable units AA members
separate themselves from other people. This is not just done physically
at closed meetings but linguistically. 'AA talk' cuts members off from
non-members and this 'verbal symbol of group cohesion' (AA 1975) is

recognised as 'special' and different from the language of outsiders or 'ordinary people':

> I'm trying to make this sound not like I would talk at an AA meeting, 'cos often it comes over a bit different. I don't want to treat you like an AA member − that's what I'm getting at. I want to treat you like a friend.
> I expect that as you sat down to table in an informal gathering, having coffee, and somebody sat down, they would treat you like a member and start talking AA to you.
> I went off to some friends who I'd phoned in advance. I went to see some people, other than AA. That was quite a good evening. It was two different worlds again. I went from one to the other. It was a straight contrast from AA type talking and general talking to ordinary people.

The anonymity tradition helps members to emphasise what is shared; their alcoholic problem, and play down the things which separate them: last names, origins, and the assumption that help or support is related to outside standards or positions: 'He said to me "Good Lord, I was a colonel in the army. I'm not taking that". I said, "Oh God it doesn't matter if you were a captain or whatever". I said, "I missed the call-up". I said, "We're all the same" '.

Formal AA talk such as 'the story', recurrent themes and concerns, and particular devices such as only using first names all help to separate AA members and their problems from outsiders. Literature, pamphlets, 'informal directives' and recommendations from conference and the GSO all aim to 'keep the member on course'. These together with routine activities, involvement and time-related tasks, allow members to operate the AA programme by constructing a way of life which is a complex of helping and being helped in the short term. Problems are always cropping up and they have to be handled quickly before they assume sufficiently large proportions to threaten the member's sobriety.

> I found that on Saturday afternoon, I had all the feelings I had when I was drinking. I don't mean on the drink, literally drinking, but the mental side. It all came back for different reasons. I went out and walked back here. I was in a real bad way. I just crumbled. I felt very lonely . . . It was a long and very lonely weekend. I don't often feel that but I did. Monday, my brother came over with his wife and

we played Monopoly. Tuesday, Graham (sponsee) came over for a meal. I phoned him Monday and said either Monday or Tuesday. He was tied up Monday, so we made it Tuesday. So I organised my brother to come over here Monday, Graham Tuesday. *It was all nasty conjuring tricks to keep everything going.* So he came over here for a couple of hours and we had a meal. Then after he went at eight o'clock I went off to some friends who I'd phoned in advance.

But as well as the short-term techniques; the 'nasty conjuring tricks', the self-help process of Alcoholics Anonymous offers a continuity of concern. It is the member's feelings of concern for others and knowledge of others' concern for him which underpins the short-term projects:

I think in a way it's the companionship, compassion, call it what you like . . . They saw me through the rough times. They didn't just drop me in the good times. Continuity. Somebody there all the time and I found this concern. I think I got let down so long while I was drinking. It was all little bits here, little bits there. But now they see things through. It's a genuine concern. A common concern.

The major themes discussed in this chapter so far, friendship, involvement, the importance of time and a continuity of concern are all part of the self-help process of groups like Alcoholics Anonymous. By using the AA method members are able to handle not just their drinking but their living. Because, for AA members, stopping drinking is only part of sobriety.

AA is not dealing with the problem of alcoholism. It's dealing with people. This is important. Quite often after a person has started to get something out of being abstinent from alcohol he feels he may want to talk about things. Abstinence is all it is at first. It isn't sobriety by any means. It's just not having a drink of booze *but you are far from sober.*

Even without drink it might be difficult to be 'sober':

Drink doesn't come into it. It's just problems of living. I find I have to listen about recovery because it's living now that for me can be a problem. It's not drinking or wanting a drink. . . Drinking doesn't mean a thing. Drinking doesn't come into anything I do or say. It's just living. Drinking has long gone. It is coping with day-to-day living.

This is where self-help groups like AA really come into their own. They are misunderstood if they are seen merely as forums for handling the specific problem which is the ostensible focus of the group's concern.

Alcoholics Anonymous and Conventional Help

The strength of self-help as against conventional help is that it provides a context within which members can handle any problem of everyday living. Members of Gamblers Anonymous report using the 'just for today' programme to help give up smoking, Weight Watchers say that their members have used the basic method to get on in their jobs. Groups like AA provide members with a perspective on life and a perspective on themselves. The skills and personal qualities which are needed to do the routine tasks in AA are used outside the group. People learn by being involved in AA and are changed by being involved. Self-help group activities – doing things for other people – enable the members to demonstrate to themselves that they can handle the problem and, most important, be a person with something to offer. This is the hidden agenda and distinguishes the 'self-helped' from the person who is helped by conventional helpers.

In conventional problem-solving, help is provided episodically. It is almost always given at the request of the person who needs the help. The general assumption behind the health and social services is that they should be drawn on in times of need, but that most people are generally problem-free and will only occasionally have difficulties of sufficient magnitude to require professional help.

For people in self-help groups like AA, however, this is not enough. Given that AA see their problem as a full-time concern, then help has to be available full time too. This is what members gain so much from; the idea that self-help is always available and available without delay. There is immense satisfaction in knowing that in the 'rough times' there is someone available who knows what it is like, who understands and who is willing to help.

Self-help helping is not restricted to certain hours of the day, by places in the queue or by the pounds in your pocket. It is immediate, and it is free. 'That's the wonderful thing about AA,' said the General Secretary, 'there is nothing I would want, no sort of advice or anything that I can't pick up the phone and have it professionally, free of charge'.

Not only is self-help helping available, but feeling that it is there is encouraged. This is done by offering unsolicited help rather than waiting to be asked for it. Again this contrasts with conventional help where it would be considered quite extraordinary for a GP to phone his patients out of the blue to ask how they felt. In conventional help it is special and significant to ask for help. Partly this is because the responsibility for helping always rests with the person who needs help and also because the person is well aware of the restricted resources with which the professional services operate. But the significance in asking for help is accentuated by the separation between the helper and the helped in terms of expertise, social position and situation. Professional help is outside the normal run of life. It is a separate and special relationship.

In self-help helping the helping is not separated off; it is part of the member's way of life. It is not a significant thing to ask for help. No appointments have to be made and there are no 'appropriate times' to phone or call, no 'appropriate channels' to go through and no receptionists barring the way to the person who gives the help. Self-help is given with pleasure when asked for and offered spontaneously when not. There is no specialised knowledge possessed by the helper which is jealously guarded from the helped. Those who are helpers are also friends, since the helping relationship is a friendship relationship. Being friends is the context within which helping takes place. There is no distinction between the treater and the treated. All have problems, all are helpers. Because of this integration of helping and being helped, problem-solvers and problem-sufferers, problem-solvers and friends, self-help helping merges into the everyday life of the self-help group members. Self-help becomes a way of life.

Although self-help helping is integrated into the everyday life of the member it is always separated off from activities with non-members. When members attempt to expand their AA life into other situations then they can get into difficulties both at the personal level with other, non-AA, individuals and at a broader social level with other organisations or groups.

At a personal level, members get into difficulties when they attempt to operate the AA method with non-members. We saw earlier how many alcoholics are put off by being 'pestered' by 'holy Joes' who want to 'rope everybody in to AA'. 'They just can't leave well alone. They are always trying to get us to go to their meetings and tell them all the gory details, well I won't. What I've done is my business and not theirs'. But apart from being rejected at Twelfth Stepping, AA members often annoy other people with their devotion to the fellowship. This causes difficulties in very many families where great concern is shown to a newcomer in AA, but little concern over family members in the house. There are many wives who preferred their drinking husbands to their AA husbands.

> At least when he was drinking I could look forward to the times when he was sober. Now with all this AA stuff he just ignores me and gets all his enjoyment from being big daddy to a series of other people while I'm left here to be mother, father and everything else to our children, I don't know how much longer I'm going to stand for it.

At a broader social level AA members can get into difficulties if they attempt to go beyond the mutual self-help which other organisations and helpers have come to understand and accept.

Mowrer (1976) describes how the members of one local AA group in America rented a small, rather dilapidated house, which they wanted as an informal 'club house' and place where they could provide temporary lodging for recovering or unemployed alcoholics. This small operation prospered and so a few of the AA group members bought a larger house, independently incorporated it and built on the original activities of the smaller house. At this point, the local office of the State Department of Mental Health offered funds to help finance this expanded operation, and the process of further funding and expansion went on until there were five houses employing a dozen or so staff. Then, the Department of Mental Health, which had encouraged and fostered the development of similar facilities in other communities, began to talk about 'operating standards' and 'accreditation requirements'. The principles and policies of AA, and people who had found sobriety by following them, were no longer considered to be sufficient for running the agency and so various staff positions were created that could only be filled by suitable professionals. As a result the AA staff members resigned, local AA support disappeared and the agencies 'were left in the hands of members of the various professions for whom, until AA came along, alcoholism was "incurable" '.

This episode could be read as just an unfortunate example of what can happen when people of goodwill get together to marry up specific initiatives and expertise with public money and organisation. Perhaps these AA members should have known better, since the AA seventh tradition states that every group 'ought to be fully self-supporting, declining outside contributions'.

From Mowrer's account the final outcome of the 'club house' venture seemed inevitable, and given the attitude of many professionals and government agencies toward self-help it is easy to see why. Even those who are very sympathetic to self-help, as they understand it, tend unthinkingly to operate from a position that is dramatically opposed to the basic principles of self-help. Nevertheless, as one wide-ranging review of self-help groups pointed out (Traunstein and Steinman 1973), at least one in three had been set up in close co-operation with professionals, although the nature of the relationship between self-help and professionals varies from group to group.

Alcoholics Anonymous have worked out a clear position on their official relationship with the professions. In a pamphlet 'designed primarily for the information of physicians', *Alcoholics Anonymous and the Medical Profession* (1955), they acknowledge that 'without the support and encouragement of sympathetic doctors AA might never have survived its first crucial years' and conclude: 'It would be unrealistic to suggest that the AA program, represented by the recovered alcoholic, is the only answer for the man or woman with a drinking problem.' Their experience suggests that the recovery of an alcoholic is most likely to be realised when two other 'elements' in addition to AA are present: 'Medicine, with its increasingly successful techniques for healing both body and mind . . . and the special power and insight that is given to those who acknowledge the importance of spiritual powers in daily living.'

This 'separate-but-compatible' view of self-help groups and the professions is not shared by all groups. For some, it is precisely because the medical profession could not, or would not, deal appropriately with them or their problems that helping themselves is so important. Most women's self-health groups are not just 'picking up the pieces' or providing peripheral support to the professional services, they are trying to change the nature of the medical enterprise. The core issue is control, from learning enough about one's own body and so demystifying the processes of health and illness, to working for a radical change in the conventional helping services so that when a particular expertise is needed, as it always will be, it will be geared to the conditions, priorities and expectations of those who receive it. 'This', says Nancy MacKeith (1975), 'is such a fundamental threat to doctors' usual ways of thinking of themselves that I believe it explains a lot about their attitude towards women wanting complete health care'.

In spite of its official position on its relationship with other professionals Alcoholics Anonymous often undermines its usefulness by pushing for groups to be set up in medical and penal institutes of various kinds. While this is, on the one hand, an important way of 'carrying the message' to those who, by definition, are likely to need to hear it, the very worst way of being introduced to AA or to any other self-help group is by being pressurised to do so, particularly by those who make it an informal condition of treatment, or use it as a marker of co-operation, motivation, or 'good behaviour'.

> We were all herded into a bus every Wednesday evening and shunted along to the local AA group. And it never dealt with my problems. They didn't talk about alcohol at all. As alcohol was all I could think about I used to shut myself off from the long mumbling speeches given by a terrible old bore who looked as if he could do with a drink. I dismissed the whole idea as useless.

Another member who was taken to AA as an informal condition of treatment, 'they never say you *have* to go, but you know that they'll say you have no commitment if you don't', did not get anything from the weekly AA meetings while he was in hospital, because 'all they seemed to talk about was drink':

> It was the sole topic of conversation and it depressed me. They talked about your difficulties but they didn't help you with them. All they did was talk about them. But it always seemed to get back to the other thing – drink. They didn't say to me, 'Why do you drink?' All they said was, 'You shouldn't drink. Don't drink'. They didn't ask me, 'Have you got any problems? Can we help you?' Probably I'd have still have been going if they'd have said, 'Now, how can we help you?' It could have been anything. I could have been worried about the rent or something. They could have advised me to go to a tribunal or something but they didn't. So I said to myself, 'That's it, they're not doing any good'.

If, like this man, newcomers do not recognise that self-help groups *can* handle the whole range of everyday living problems, as well as 'the' problem, then they may not see the real value of staying with the group and 'becoming a member'. On the other hand, being taken to AA as a condition of treatment is hardly likely to be conducive to the development of the kind of friendships and new sets of relationships which becoming a member of a group like AA involves.

Many professionals feel threatened by the rapid growth of the self-help movement. Many others, recognising the value of various self-help enterprises, have proposed that professionals should become directly involved. Vattano (1972), for example, claims that there are certain functions the professional is 'uniquely equipped to perform'; a major one being to act as a 'catalyst and facilitator' in the early stages. Mowrer (1971), too, felt that professionals could set up self-help groups and suggested that universities should 'train and supply persons competent to perform this type of function'. Jertson (1975), like many others, rightly thinks such enthusiasm should be tempered, since it presents a number of problems that the 'facilitators' ought to be aware of. Professional involvement will 'contribute to a loss of that one value uniquely cherished by the self-help group; the perceived ability to help itself'.

Changes in AA

Alcoholics Anonymous is a well-established, well thought of, worldwide organisation whose essence is an agreed programme of recovery which enables alcoholics to deconstruct their problems and reconstruct their lives. Adherence to the basic programme is necessary if members are to recover, while maintaining the steps and traditions, which embody the programme and its philosophy, is the main task of the General Service Board and a personal responsibility of all AA members.

In spite of this, Alcoholics Anonymous is not a static organisation. It develops in response to changing needs and circumstances. For example, roughly twenty per cent of its groups in England and Wales are new each year while twenty per cent of the members have been in the fellowship for less than a year. Given this constant change and development it was not surprising to find that a large proportion of current members said that they would like to see further changes in the way AA operates. Table 5.4 shows that this desire for change was not something felt only by newcomers who might not have 'fully understood' what the programme meant.

The range of possible changes which members mentioned was wide, but there were two main sets of proposals, the first concerning the organisation of meetings and the second questioning the fellowship's position on publicity and anonymity.

Some of the suggested changes in relation to meetings reflected members' views on 'unhelpful' stories. They said there should be less

Table 5.4: Desire for Change in AA and Years in AA

Desire for change	Under 2		2 < 6		6 or more		Total	
	N	%	N	%	N	%	N	%
Yes	24	38.7	19	37.3	23	39.7	66	38.6
No	27	43.5	28	54.9	31	53.4	86	50.3
Don't know	11	17.7	4	7.8	4	6.9	19	11.1
Total	62		51		58		171	

'drunkalogues' and more emphasis on the recovery part of the programme. Many members suggested changes in the way meetings are run. In particular, various members felt that there should be more control over the meeting from the chairman, especially in respect of speakers who talk for too long and those who are drunk or disruptive. A few proposed that a maximum time limit should be set for speakers and 30 minutes seemed popular. Others saw 'quickies' as a solution so that everyone would have a chance to speak. One member suggested that there could be a show of hands at the beginning of the meeting to determine who wanted to speak. This, it was felt, would cover those members with problems uppermost in their mind.

Discussion groups were popular with many members. Some, in large groups, suggested that meetings should break up into smaller groups especially for newcomers or for those who could not talk to large numbers of people, while a few members suggested there should be a theme for the day. Several members would like to see newcomers encouraged to be more active and it was also felt they should be given more friendship and 'love'. One member suggested they be given a card with a few telephone numbers as soon as they arrive. Newcomers were said to need some kind of protection from the rigid domineering attitudes of some longstanding members. However, it was emphasised, by lots of members, that meetings should always have a majority of people who had been sober for a period of time.

Surprising, perhaps, was the suggestion by a number of members that there should be more 'open meetings' to be attended by outside 'experts' such as doctors, probation officers, psychiatrists and social workers who could 'find out about what we are' and also 'give us the benefit of their advice about alcoholism'.

The change which was mentioned most often, by twenty per cent of the sample, was the proposal to relax AA's anonymity in order to give the fellowship more publicity. Publicity was felt to be necessary for three reasons: to inform the general public about alcoholism as a disease and thereby 'remove the stigma'; to inform professionals, especially doctors, about the disease and how AA helps; and thirdly, to inform suffering alcoholics and so remove the mysticism surrounding the fellowship and make it more accessible. Some wanted the publicity to come from GSO, several suggested making far more use of radio, TV, press and yellow pages, while some wanted to remove the personal anonymity rules in order to help to publicise the role of the fellowship. These views, held by a large number of AA members, are clearly at variance with basic AA principles. The eleventh tradition of AA states: 'Our public relations policy is based on attraction rather than promotion; we need always maintain personal anonymity at the level of press, radio and films' while the twelfth tradition emphasis that, 'Anonymity is the spiritual foundation of our traditions, ever reminding us to place principles before personalities'.

Anonymity has been a central principle of AA from its very early days. But in the beginning anonymity 'was not born of confidence, it was the child of our early fears' (AA 1952b). When the big book, *Alcoholics Anonymous*, appeared in 1939 its foreword carried this revealing statement:

> It is important that we remain anonymous because we are too few, at present to handle the overwhelming number of personal appeals which may result from this publication. Being mostly business or professional folk, we could not well carry on our occupations in such an event.

It is easy to see the fear in that passage.

As AA grew so did the anonymity and publicity problem. Many members who had achieved a period of sobriety wanted to tell others about themselves, their changed life and the wonders of Alcoholics Anonymous which had enabled it all to happen. With generous and genuine concern for drinking alcoholics they wanted everyone to know about AA so that there could be no excuse for someone to go on drinking in ignorance of what AA was and what it had to offer. As AA (1952b) put it

> With characteristic intemperance, however, some of our newcomers cared not at all for secrecy. They wanted to shout AA from the housetops, and did. Alcoholics barely dry rushed about bright

eyed, buttonholing anyone who would listen to their stories. Others hurried to place themselves before microphones and cameras . . . They had changed from AA members to AA show-offs.

This phenomenon of early growth set the fellowship thinking seriously about how anonymous an AA member should be. 'Our growth made it plain that we couldn't be a secret society, but it was equally plain that we couldn't be a vaudeville act either.' Spreading the good news, by word of mouth, helped the recovering alcoholic to lose his fear of alcoholic stigma and enabled those he met to understand what AA was and how it worked. This, although 'not in the strict letter of anonymity' was 'well within its spirit'. But it soon became apparent that word-of-mouth publicity was too limited.

The real test of the anonymity principle came to AA in the early 1940s when several major pieces of press publicity, plus the famous Jack Alexander article in the *Saturday Evening Post* (1941), made AA a national institution. Magazines wanted AA stories, film companies wanted to record the 'good news', radio and television companies wanted personal appearances by people who had remained sober the AA way.

> As the tide offering top public approval swept in, we realized that it could do us incalculable good or great harm. Everything would depend upon how it was channelled. We simply couldn't afford to take the chance of letting self-appointed members present them-selves as messiahs representing AA before the whole public. The promoter instinct in us might be our undoing. If even one publicly got drunk, or was lured into using AA's name for his own purposes, the damage might be irreparable (AA 1952b).

The decision was to 'put principles before personalities' and, because the dangers of one slip ruining everything were so great, to demand one hundred per cent anonymity.

This decision to sacrifice individual publicity for that of the fellow-ship and its principles paid off handsomely. It resulted in 'more favourable publicity of Alcoholics Anonymous than could possibly have been obtained through all the arts and abilities of AA's best press agency'. In the beginning the press were baffled, but gradually got the point that 'Here was something rare in the world — a society which said it wished to publicise its principles and its work, but not its individual members'.

Debates about the usefulness of the anonymity tradition have continued ever since. Every so often a member 'breaks ranks' and goes public to 'carry the message' of AA on the strength of his own experiences. A recent example was Lord Kimberley, under a seven-column headline in the *Daily Mail* (1976) which read 'Champagne from a tin mug on my crazy road to ruin'. After relating his drinking history, his discovery of AA and the fact that he had not had a drink for four years he concluded:

> There remains a great barrier between the organisation and the general public. This is because it clings to its original tradition of anonymity, which was deemed necessary forty years ago, but today, in my opinion, hinders its work in many instances. I feel most strongly that if Alcoholics Anonymous does not move with the times it will continue to deal only with the chronic alcoholics and will make little impression on a person afflicted in the early stages of the illness.

Clearly this view is shared by many members of AA and the anonymity and publicity issue will continue to be hotly debated.

General Service Office is very sensitive to any degree of criticism. When the results of the present survey were conveyed to them, as part of the natural process of reporting back to those who were the subject of the survey, the demands for change and the desire on the part of many members for changes in the publicity and anonymity policy were dismissed on the grounds that people who held such views would be likely to be newcomers who had not yet fully appreciated the core principles and philosophy of the fellowship.

Table 5.5: Desire for Less Anonymity/More Publicity and 'Involvement' in AA

'Involvement'	Members who want less anonymity/ more publicity (N = 35) %	Other members (N = 134) %	Total (N = 169) %
Been secretary	45.7	44.8	45.0
Been an intergroup representative	51.4	43.0	44.7
Been a sponsor	54.3	50.7	51.5
Been in AA over 2 years	62.9	64.0	63.7

In fact, as Table 5.5 shows, members who wanted these changes were just as active and longstanding in the fellowship as anyone else.

Other aspects of the AA programme which some members felt could be changed included giving less emphasis to the 'spiritual side' of the activity, developing a more liberal attitude to God and doing away with 'religious mania'. Increases in the level of twelfth-step work and sponsorship were very popular and some suggested there ought to be more local social activities. Certain aspects of AA structure were felt to be in need of change. Members felt that there should be 'more understanding between rank and file and Head Office'; more group to group co-operation, especially on twelfth stepping, and 'less committees and intergroups' which were seen by one member as 'just collecting together people who like running things'.

Taken together, the great majority of changes which members would like to see in AA are quite consistent with the core feature of AA as 'a way of life' which was described earlier in this chapter. The general theme of change is for AA to demand more of the members, to be more linked to outside organisations and professionals, to involve more people, to be more expansive, to have more activities, to be more flexible, to cater for the needs of as wide a cross-section of people as possible, to stress even more the social as well as problematic aspects of life. Those who want more publicity and less anonymity are, in a sense, carrying the basic realities of the self-help process of AA to their natural conclusions. They have, indeed, incorporated 'being an alcoholic' into their everyday view of themselves; they have made being in AA their way of life. To them, then, it is incongruous to deny in public what they are and why they are. The 'sacrifice' involved in anonymity is too great.

This chapter has attempted to show how Alcoholics Anonymous requires a high degree of active involvement from its members. Alcoholics Anonymous is not just a matter of passive participation in a helping process. Nor is it simply a matter of *doing*. It is a matter of *being*; of being in the group, and of being in AA outside of the group, during the ordinary everyday life of the member. This is what is meant when people say that self-help is a way of life, and this is why Alcoholics Anonymous requires its members to change into almost completely different people if they are to handle their alcoholism the AA·way.

6 CONCLUSION

> Throughout history deprived members of society have frequently banded together to improve their lot or to seek 'justice' as they perceive it... The active alcoholic person's anguish may be harder to bear than that of most other persecuted groups... After affiliation with AA, however, the alcoholic person discovers that he is not a unique phenomenon and that there are others like him who are not only willing to help but have shared his feelings of helplessness, alienation and terror. Within AA, the strong union among members produced by a common history of emotional and social deprivation has led to the belief that only one alcoholic person can understand another. (Madsen 1974)

There is a wide measure of agreement among medical professionals, the general public, government agencies and various social work and other helping groups that Alcoholics Anonymous has had significant success with enabling large numbers of people to cope with their severe alcoholism.

Even those who are critical of various aspects of the Alcoholics Anonymous programme of recovery or the fellowship's attitude toward other treatments or its influence in the alcoholism field rarely hesitate to confirm the empirical fact of its large number of successes. Further recognition of the support given to AA is evident in the fact that many hospitals, clinics, prisons and industrial firms welcome and encourage the formation of AA groups within their own organisations. The effect of AA extends far beyond its members and their families. AA has been a force for social change, it has dramatised alcoholism as an illness, substituted 'alcoholic' for 'drunkard' in public thinking with all that that implies for the social and moral standing of the individual, and demonstrated that, despite its seeming intractability, something could be done about alcoholism.

An analysis of the precise role of AA in the change of public attitudes toward those with drinking problems and the influence of the fellowship on psychiatry and other branches of medicine has yet to be written. It would be a mammoth task, as would be the compilation of a systematic account of the foundation, spread and development of AA into its present position as an international organisation with well over a million members. But these are not the only unanswered questions about Alcoholics Anonymous. There are many thousands of people who are as mystified as they are delighted by the fact that their relations, friends, workmates and acquaintances became able to control their chronic alcoholism after contact with AA. The aim of this book, therefore, has been to throw some light on the self-help process of Alcoholics Anonymous and to show something of the way in which members of the fellowship talk themselves out of their alcoholism.

Becoming a member of AA can take many forms and individual careers prior to coming into contact with the fellowship can be very different from each other. Some people know a great deal about AA and keep it 'in mind' for when they reach a point when nothing else will help, others know nothing about AA and are pressurised to attend a meeting by concerned relations or by professional helpers who consider AA as part of their therapeutic repertoire. But whatever the pathway, the crucial time for an active alcoholic is when he comes to realise, for whatever reasons, that people in AA know what he is like, know his problems, understand how he feels, have been through it all themselves and have 'come out at the other side'.

This process of identification takes place at twelfth-step contacts, at meetings where the alcoholic hears the 'stories' and partly it can come about through reading the voluminous AA literature. The confirmation of the potential member's identification with AA and its members comes when the newcomer admits, in public, that he is 'an alcoholic'. At this point the sense of relief can be enormous. But the relief is not a relief which comes from knowing that he has *got* 'alcoholism', but from knowing that he *is* 'an alcoholic'. Because the whole of the self-help process of Alcoholics Anonymous is not a matter of solving problems: it is a matter of changing people. And once the newcomer takes himself to be 'an alcoholic', with all that that means in AA in terms of their simple disease model of alcoholism and its corollary, that the newcomer can never drink again, then the process of talking himself out of his alcoholism can begin.

Talking is the key to AA. Everybody talks and everybody enjoys it immensely. Some people find it difficult but everybody knows how important it is, because it is only through talk, and AA's special kind of talking, that 'newcomers' can share and understand what AA is and 'old timers' can carry the AA message to those they think should hear it.

Talking, however, is not just for telling other people what you are like or for explaining what AA is and what it does to active alcoholics or outsiders. AA talking is the mechanism for members to gradually separate themselves from their past and confirm their new persona as an AA member. As time goes by talk and stories change. The emphasis of the story, and through this the status of the teller of the story, changes from drinking experiences and drinking problems to recovery, involvement in AA and the restructuring of everyday life.

For although alcohol and drinking problems are the things which brought the members together the thing which keeps them together and separated from 'the problem' is their involvement in the activities of the fellowship. This enables them to build up their self-esteem and construct a life of sobriety, rather than just abstinence.

A sober life means a life in which members follow the AA method of working towards short-term targets and are supported by a continuity of concern. Help and helping become everyday features of the member's life. In AA, as in other self-help groups, the separation between helper and helped is bridged. All are helpers and all are helped. No one need be afraid to ask for help because, unlike professional help, it is always available, given with pleasure and by someone who understands exactly what it is like. But while certain bridges are built others are broken down. AA emphasises things which are shared but enables members to play down things which separate them; last names, origins, and the assumption that help or support is related to outside standards or positions. Members separate themselves from drinking and also from past friends, locations and ways of behaving. AA friends take over and AA activities become a central part of the member's life.

As time goes by some members grow out of AA. They do not attend meetings and do not take any part in the formal parts of the fellowship. And yet these people, arguably the 'real' successes of AA, have learned how to cope not only with their drinking problem, but with themselves. Through the activities of the group and through the relationships and friendships which they formed, they have changed as people. They can handle not only their drinking problem but, by operating the AA method, themselves and their lives. AA for them has really become a way of life. It has enabled them to talk themselves out of alcoholism, their previous way of life.

Not everyone who comes into contact with Alcoholics Anonymous progresses to a life of sobriety, quite apart from those many alcoholics who would not go near AA if you paid them. The question of how successful AA is in comparison with other responses to alcoholism is often asked but never answered. The lack of answer is not because people are not interested in finding out, or do not care what the answer is, but because there is no way of finding out. There is no way of doing a controlled comparative study since no one would be able technically to determine the universe of alcoholics from which to draw the samples for comparison, and no one would be able ethically to assign alcoholics to either AA or another 'therapy' since an essential feature of becoming an AA member is that the decision is, for whatever reason and with whatever information or commitment, made by the individual involved.

But the question of 'success', or rather 'how successful in comparison with other therapies', has taken up too much space in the literature on Alcoholics Anonymous. Not enough time has been spent trying to understand how AA succeeded with those people it succeeded with. This has been the aim of the present book. It is hoped that by presenting a clear picture of the self-help process of Alcoholics Anonymous that those who have some kind of alcohol problem and who think that AA might have something to offer will make a better informed decision. In addition, it is hoped that the book will be of value to all those professionals and other helpers who so readily praise AA and encourage their clients and patients to attend without really knowing what happens there, what a newcomer is expected to do or in what way being in AA is suitable for the person in question or in what way the self-help process of AA is compatible with their own professional involvement with the alcoholic. For AA is not just a remedy which one can take down from the shelf and try for a while. AA demands much more of its members than that. It demands their involvement, their commitment, and it aims to change them as people. In some cases it succeeds magnificently, in others it is a dismal failure. As Griffith Edwards (1964) concluded at the end of his article on the puzzle of AA: 'If we could understand AA we should in the process come to understand a great deal about human interaction'.

APPENDIX: THE SURVEY OF AA IN ENGLAND AND WALES

The survey of Alcoholics Anonymous in England and Wales was conducted in the first week of November 1976. This appendix contains:
1. the covering letter sent by Bill, the General Secretary of AA, to the Secretaries of the random sample of fifty groups included in the survey,
2. the introductory letter from the Addiction Research Unit setting out the aims of the survey and the mechanics of its administration, and
3. the questionnaires which one in four of the members of each of the fifty survey groups was asked to complete.

Completed questionnaires were returned from forty-three of the fifty groups. Two of the remaining seven groups had ceased to exist in the time between the drawing of the samples from the most up-to-date information at the General Service Office and the survey week. Nothing at all was heard from the other five groups any or all of which may either have folded or decided to have nothing to do with the study.

ALCOHOLICS ANONYMOUS STERLING AREA SERVICES.

GENERAL SERVICE OFFICE

18th October, 1976.

Dear Friend,

I am sure that you will find the attached letter from David Robinson, the Senior Lecturer at the Institute of Psychiatry self explanatory.

At a first glance the questionnaire appears to be lengthy, but in actual fact answering the questions is relatively simple — merely circling a number against a particular reply.

The final collated results will be supplied to us, and in due course published within the Fellowship.

It is felt that this exercise will produce information not previously available to us, and that we will be able to put it to good use.

Should you have any queries please do not hesitate to contact me — in the meantime every good wish to all our friends in the group.

Yours sincerely,

General Secretary.

UNIVERSITY OF LONDON
BRITISH POSTGRADUATE MEDICAL FEDERATION

THE BETHLEM ROYAL HOSPITAL
AND
THE MAUDSLEY HOSPITAL

DEPARTMENT OF PSYCHIATRY

INSTITUTE OF PSYCHIATRY

Dear Secretary,

A.   RESEARCH ON SELF-HELP

Over the past two years my colleague Dr. Stuart Henry and I have been collecting together a great deal of written material dealing with, and produced by, literally hundreds of different self-help groups and organisations both here and abroad. In addition, we have been interviewing members of various groups, going to group meetings and participating with members in a whole range of group activities. As you can imagine we now have a great mass of field notes, tape-recorded interviews and personal impressions to add to the 'library' of books, pamphlets, newsletters and other written material. I hope, also, that we have a rather clearer idea, than when we began, about what the very rapidly growing self-help movement is all about.

In the second stage of our research we are narrowing the scope of our interest in order to concentrate on a small number (12-15) of particular self-help groups and organisations. Among the ones we are looking at are, for example, Weightwatchers, The Phobics Society, Gamblers Anonymous, Relatives of the Depressed, and so on. And the reason we want to concentrate on a small number of groups is in order to get a rather more representative coverage of members' ideas and experiences. Up to now we have spent our time talking to leaders, founders, National Secretaries and so on. But while this is absolutely vital at the outset we now need to get a better feel of the organisation as a whole, so we need to question a representative sample of members up and down the country.

The reason we are writing to you now is that we would like to have Alcoholics Anonymous as one of the self-help groups we look at in greater detail. This is not merely because we work in an Addiction Research Unit, but because A.A. is readily acknowledged to be the model self-help group: long established, operating world-wide, successful, copied by newer groups, widely discussed, known to the general public and to the professions alike, and so on.

As you can see from the covering letter from Redcliffe Gardens we have been in contact with the general secretary about our survey and he has discussed both it and the questionnaire with the Executive Committee who have given it the go-ahead. However, this support by the Executive Committee is not just an academic nicety as far as we are concerned, it is much more than that. Because if this survey is to be of any value, it must be seen as covering issues and topics which members feel are important and central to A.A. activity. The fact that the Executive Committee was interested in the questionnaire and keen to be provided with the findings - which we are, of course, delighted to do - makes us believe that the survey deals with at least some central A.A. concerns. We very much hope that a sample of members from the group of which you are secretary will agree to take part and complete our questionnaire.

continued ...

B.   THE A.A. SURVEY

1.   The A.A. survey will take place during one particular week, 1st - 7th
     November 1976.

2.   We have drawn a random sample of 50 A.A. groups from the whole of England
     and Wales and yours is one of those which was selected.

3.   A packet of questionnaires will be sent to you, as group secretary,
     a few days before the survey week.

4.   The questionnaires should be given out at the regular A.A. meeting
     during the survey week 1st-7th November 1976.

5.   The questionnaires should be completed and returned to you at that same
     meeting.

6.   There will be a stamped and addressed envelope so that you can send
     all completed questionnaires back to me here at the Addiction Research Unit.

C.   WHO FILLS IN THE A.A. QUESTIONNAIRE?

a)   The general principle: Ideally we would like to interview every member of
     every group in England and Wales. Clearly, in terms of time and money this
     is impossible. Our statisticians here at the Institute have said that if we
     take a random sample of 50 groups and then take 1 in 4 people within those
     groups we shall get an adequately representative sample of A.A. members. This,
     then, is what we are doing. This means that we shall get a real cross-section
     of members, young-old, new-old timers, men-women, office holders and not; etc.
     etc. As you will appreciate it is absolutely vital that the selection is done
     properly so that we don't just get the senior, experienced, most interested
     people giving their views. The whole survey will be quite valueless if we do.
     We must get a cross-section of the complete membership when we put all the
     50 group samples together.

b)   Selecting the 1 in 4 samples of members from your group

1.   In the packet which we shall send you before the survey week will be
     the questionnaires and, in addition;
                         (i) A MEMBER CHART
                         (ii) A CODE ENVELOPE

2.   In brief, the procedure is as follows:
     a) Write down in ALPHABETICAL ORDER OF CHRISTIAN NAMES on the MEMBER CHART
         every person who has come to the meeting.

     b) Open the CODE ENVELOPE. In it you will find a list of CODE NUMBERS.

     c) Give a questionnaire ONLY to those people whose name falls on a line
         with one of the CODE numbers against it.

3.   A MEMBER CHART with some fake names, and some CODE NUMBERS indicating
     which people would have to fill in the questionnaire is shown on the
     next page of this letter P.3.

Continued....

MEMBER CHART	
CODE NUMBER	NAME
1	secretary
2	Alan
3	Brian
4	David
5	George A
6	George B
7	Helen
8	Margaret C
9	Margaret P
10	Norman
11	Tony
12	Trevor
13	William S
14	William Y
⋮ 30 etc.	

CODE SHEET
Give a questionnaire ONLY to people whose name falls on a line with the following CODE NUMBER against it
2. 7. 9. 14. 20. 22.....

In this example, the people who would fill in the questionnaire would be Alan, Helen, Margaret P and William Y.

I hope this is clear and that you will be able to complete our questionnaires for us. We hope also that those who do fill them in will enjoy doing so.

If anyone who is not picked for the survey would like to fill in a questionnaire then please give them one of the spare questionnaires which you will have left over after doing the selection. But PLEASE mark these questionnaires as EXTRA. We are, of course, interested in what any member has to tell us BUT for the main survey we can only use the material from the properly selected sample.

On a personal note, you will see that on the MEMBER CHART we have put SECRETARY on line 1. This means that 1 in 4 of the 50 group secretaries will be selected to fill in a questionnaire. If you are not one of them we shall be delighted to receive a questionnaire from you but PLEASE put SECRETARY EXTRA on the front page.

If you have any difficulties or queries please do not hesitate to phone us here at the Unit.

With best wishes.

Yours sincerely,

David Robinson, Ph.D.,
Senior Lecturer

Addiction Research Unit,

Institute of Psychiatry,

101 Denmark Hill,

London SE 5

Dear Member,

ALCOHOLICS ANONYMOUS QUESTIONNAIRE

This questionnaire survey forms part of a larger project concerned with mutual self-help groups. As a result of a lot of preliminary work with A.A. groups and members we feel that the questionnaire deals with some of the core aspects of A.A. activity and organisation.

The information which you provide is, of course, entirely confidential and, as you will see, no names appear on the form and we do not ask any questions about your private life. Our concern is with the fellowship of A.A. not the identification of individual members. If you have any comments on the questionnaire, or further comments on A.A. which you would like to give us, please do not hesitate to write to us at the above address.

We very much appreciate your co-operation and hope that you find the questionnaire as interesting to fill in as we did to produce.

With best wishes.

Yours sincerely,

David Robinson and Stuart Henry
Project staff

SECTION A

A Brief Outline of Your A.A. History

A1 i When did you attend your first ever A.A. meeting? 19.....

   ii Which group was that? ....

A2 i What is the name of the group where you were given

      this questionnaire? .. ..

   ii When did you first contact this group? 19.....

   iii How many meetings of this group have you gone to in the

       past four weeks? ....

A3 Which other groups have you gone to in the past four weeks?
    (PLEASE FILL IN DETAILS ON THE CHART BELOW)

	NAME OF OTHER GROUPS WHICH YOU HAVE GONE TO IN THE PAST FOUR WEEKS	NUMBER OF MEETINGS ATTENDED IN THE PAST 4 WEEKS
1		
2		
3		
4		
5		
6		
7		

A4 When you go to A.A. meetings do you usually go along alone or
    with other people? (PLEASE CIRCLE)

                          I usually go alone   1
                          About half and half   2
                          I usually go with others   3

Have you answered each question? PLEASE CHECK

A5 i Is there one particular group which you are most closely
       involved with at the moment, which you think of as your
       'base' or 'home' group?

                    (PLEASE CIRCLE)   NO   1
                                       YES   0

    ii (IF YES) Which group is that? ....

13 ☐

SECTION B

Your Early Time in A.A.

B1 Did you know about A.A. before drink began to be a
    problem? (PLEASE CIRCLE)

                    YES, I knew a lot about A.A.   1
                    YES, I knew a little about A.A.   2
                    I had only heard of A.A.   3
                    I had never heard of A.A.   4

14 ☐ T

B2 i Did anyone try to persuade you to cut down
       or stop your drinking before you went to A.A.?

                    (PLEASE CIRCLE)   NO   1
                                       YES   2

    ii (IF YES) Who tried to persuade you? (PLEASE CIRCLE ANY
                   PEOPLE WHO TRIED TO PERSUADE YOU)

                         Wife/Husband   2
                    Other family members   2
                              Friends   2
                           Work mates   2
                             Employer   2
                                 G.P.   2
             Others (PLEASE SPECIFY) ....
       ....
       ....

15 ☐ T

	16
	17
	18
	19
	20
	21
	22

Have you answered each question? PLEASE CHECK

B3 What kind of people were involved in your decision to go
   to A.A. the first time? (PLEASE CIRCLE ALL PEOPLE
                                           WHO WERE INVOLVED)

	Family	2	23
	Friends	2	24
	Employer	2	25
	G.P.	2	26
	Psychiatrist	2	27
	Social Worker	2	28
	Probation officer	2	29
Others (PLEASE SPECIFY)	A.A. member	2	30
			31

....
....

B4 How did you think A.A. could help you when you went to
   your first meeting? ....

....
....

32

B5 How many meetings did you go to in the four weeks after your

   first meeting? ....

33 34

B6 i Do you feel that you are now a real member of A.A.?

                    (PLEASE CIRCLE)   NO   1
                                         YES 2

35   T

   ii (IF NO) Why? ....

....
....
....

36

Have you answered each question? PLEASE CHECK

B7 i Have you ever 'dropped out' of A.A.? (PLEASE CIRCLE)

NO   0

YES   X

ii (IF YES) How many times have you 'dropped out'?

.... times

iii On the last occasion, how long did you 'drop out' of

A.A. for? . ...

iv Why did you drop out on that occasion? ....

....

....

v Did you start drinking heavily again? (PLEASE CIRCLE)

YES, very heavily   1

YES, quite heavily   2

I just drank a little   3

I didn't drink at all   4

vi Why did you return to A.A.? ....

....

....

B8 i Have you ever had a sponsor? (PLEASE CIRCLE)

NO   1

YES   2

ii (IF NO) Why not? ....

....

....

iii (IF YES) What especially did your sponsor

provide for you? ....

....

....

Have you answered each question? PLEASE CHECK

iv What was the most <u>unhelpful</u> thing about your

sponsor? ....

....

....

41

v How many sponsors have you got now? ....

vi Are you still in touch with your <u>original</u>

sponsor? (PLEASE CIRCLE)   YES   1

NO   2

42   T

vii (IF NO) Why not? ....

....

....

SECTION C

<u>Your A.A. Activities Now</u>

C1 What parts of A.A. group meetings do you gain most from?

(PLEASE CIRCLE ON CHART 1 HOW HELPFUL YOU FIND EACH PART OF
A.A. MEETINGS)

CHART 1

Parts of the Programme	The part was:		
	Very Helpful for me	Fairly Helpful for me	Not helpful At All for me
Discussion before the meeting	1	2	3
Hearing talks and stories	1	2	3
Giving talks and stories	1	2	3
Discussion groups	1	2	3
Discussion after the closing prayer	1	2	3
Official A.A. business	1	2	3
Other (PLEASE SPECIFY)			
....	X	X	X
....	X	X	X

43
44
45
46
47
48

49

Have you answered each question? <u>PLEASE CHECK</u>

C2 In what way would you like A.A. meetings to be improved?

....

....

....

C3 Have you ever spoken at an A.A. meeting?
    (PLEASE CIRCLE)

YES, I have spoken <u>regularly</u>	1
YES, I have spoken <u>occasionally</u>	2
I have <u>hardly</u> spoken at all	3
I have <u>never</u> spoken at all	4

C4 i Have you ever told your story at an A.A. meeting?

(PLEASE CIRCLE)	NO	1
	YES	2

    ii (IF NO) Why have you never told your story? ....

    ....

    ....

    iii (IF YES) How long after going to your first A.A. meeting
        did you <u>first</u> tell your story? ....

    iv How many times have you told your story in the past
        year? ....

     v In what way has the emphasis of your story changed since
        you first told it? ....

        ....

        ....

C5 i Roughly what proportion of <u>other people's</u> stories do

       you gain something from ?   (PLEASE CIRCLE)

All of them	1
75% of them	2
50% of them	3
25% of them	4
None of them	5

       <u>Have you answered each question?</u> <u>PLEASE CHECK</u>

ii What is it about some people's stories that you <u>don't</u>
find particularly useful? ....
....
....

C6 i Have you ever 12th stepped a newcomer? (PLEASE CIRCLE)

YES   1

NO   2

(IF NO) Why not? ....
....
....

ii Have you ever been on a 12th step call?

(PLEASE CIRCLE)   YES   1

NO   2

(IF NO) Why not? . ...
....
....

C7 i Have you ever acted as a sponsor to a new A.A. member?

(PLEASE CIRCLE)   YES   1

NO   2

ii (IF NO) Why not? ....
....
............................(GO TO QUESTION C8)

iii (IF YES) How many people have you sponsored?

.... people

iv How long after you went to your <u>first A.A. meeting</u> did
you first become a sponsor? ....

<u>Have you answered each question?</u> PLEASE CHECK

v What particularly do you gain from being a sponsor?

....

....

....

vi What particularly have you found difficult about being

a sponsor? ....

....

....

vii Are you still in touch with the person you first

sponsored? (PLEASE CIRCLE)   NO   0

                                    YES   X

(IF YES) How long does that make it you have been in

contact with the person you first sponsored? ....

C8 Have you ever gone to an A.A. convention, or mini-convention?

                        (PLEASE CIRCLE)   YES   1

                                           NO   2

C9 Have you ever attended an inter-group meeting?

                        (PLEASE CIRCLE)   YES   1

                                           NO   2

C10 Have you ever gone to an A.A. conference?

                        (PLEASE CIRCLE)   YES   1

                                           NO   2

C11 Have you ever acted as Secretary of an A.A. group?

                        (PLEASE CIRCLE)   YES   1

                                           NO   2

Have you answered each question? PLEASE CHECK

C12 Have you ever been the <u>contact person</u> of an A.A. group?

(PLEASE CIRCLE)   YES 1
NO 2

C13 Have you ever acted as <u>Treasurer</u> of any A.A. group

(PLEASE CIRCLE)   YES 1
NO 2

C14 Have you ever gone to talk to any <u>outside organisation</u>
about A.A.? (PLEASE CIRCLE)

YES 1
NO 2

(IF YES) What organisations have you spoken to within
the past year? (PLEASE LIST THEM) ....
....
....

C15 Have you ever manned a <u>switchboard</u> of the A.A. telephone
service? (PLEASE CIRCLE)

YES 1
NO 2

C16 In the past year have you read any A.A. <u>pamphlets</u>?

(PLEASE CIRCLE) YES regularly   1
YES occasionally 2
YES very rarely 3
NO 4

C17 Do you ever read <u>The Big Book</u>? (PLEASE CIRCLE)

YES regularly 1
YES occasionally 2
YES very rarely 3
NO 4

<u>Have you answered each question?</u> <u>PLEASE CHECK</u>

C18 Do you ever read <u>Share</u>? (PLEASE CIRCLE)

YES regularly	1
YES occasionally	2
YES very rarely	3
NO	4

C19 i Have you ever <u>written</u> a piece for Share?

(PLEASE CIRCLE)   YES 1

NO 2

ii (IF YES) What did you write about? ....

....

....

C20 Do you ever read <u>Box 514</u>? (PLEASE CIRCLE)

YES regularly	1
YES occasionally	2
YES very rarely	3
NO	4

C21 Do you contribute to the <u>collection</u> at A.A.

meetings? (PLEASE CIRCLE)

YES regularly	1
YES occasionally	2
YES very rarely	3
NO	4

SECTION D

Contact with other A.A.'s Outside Meetings

D1 Have you ever had other A.A.'s to <u>your</u> home? (PLEASE CIRCLE)

YES, regularly	1
YES, occasionally	2
YES, very rarely	3
NO	4

Have you answered each question? PLEASE CHECK

D2 Have you ever been to other A.A.'s homes? (PLEASE CIRCLE)

YES, regularly	1
YES, occasionally	2
YES, very rarely	3
NO	4

6

_____

D3 i Do you meet A.A.'s socially, other than at

    private homes? (PLEASE CIRCLE)   NO 0

                                             YES X

    ii (IF YES) What kind of places or occasions do you

        meet other A.A.'s socially (PLEASE SPECIFY)

        ....

        ....

        ....

7

_____

D4 Do you ever meet other A.A.'s at your place of work?

(PLEASE CIRCLE)	YES, regularly	1
	YES, occasionally	2
	YES, very rarely	3
	NO, I do not work	4
	NO, I work but don't meet other A.A.'s	5

8 T

_____

D5 Have you made any new friends in A.A.? (PLEASE CIRCLE)

YES, a lot	1
YES, a few	2
NO	3

9 T

_____

D6 Do you still see the friends you had before you

began coming to A.A.? (PLEASE CIRCLE)

Most of them	1
Some of them	2
Hardly any of them	3
None of them	4

10 T

_____

Have you answered each question? PLEASE CHECK

D7 Do you feel that social meetings between A.A.'s outside A.A.

   meetings is part of the A.A. programme? (PLEASE CIRCLE)

YES, an <u>essential</u> part of the programme	1
YES, a <u>useful</u> part of the programme	2
NO, it's <u>quite separate</u> from the programme	3

SECTION E

Your Problem and How A.A. Has Helped

E1 i How many of the following physical problems have you
      experienced? (PLEASE CIRCLE <u>ALL</u> PROBLEMS YOU HAVE HAD,
      <u>AND</u> EACH PERIOD IN WHICH YOU HAD THEM)

Physical Problems	Experienced the problem:		
	Before AA	Since First AA Meeting	In Past 4 weeks
Severe morning shakes	1	2	4
'Blackouts' after drinking	1	2	4
D.T.'s	1	2	4
'Heard voices'	1	2	4
'Seen things'	1	2	4
Been too drunk to stand up	1	2	4
Others (PLEASE SPECIFY)			
....	X	X	X
....	X	X	X

      ii Which was the worst of these <u>physical</u> problems for YOU?

      ....

      ....

      iii Do you feel that your physical health has improved

         since being in A.A.? (PLEASE CIRCLE)

YES, a great deal	1
YES, a little	2
NO, not at all	3

Have you answered each question? <u>PLEASE CHECK</u>

E2　i　How many of the following <u>mental</u> problems have you
experienced?　(PLEASE CIRCLE <u>ALL</u> PROBLEMS YOU HAVE HAD,
<u>AND</u> EACH PERIOD IN WHICH YOU HAD THEM)

Mental Problems	Experienced the problem:		
	Before <u>AA</u>	Since First <u>AA Meeting</u>	In Past <u>4 Weeks</u>
Felt extremely frightened	1	2	4
Tried to commit suicide	1	2	4
Felt deep shame	1	2	4
Felt unable to trust anyone	1	2	4
Felt uncontrollable anger	1	2	4
Felt extremely depressed	1	2	4
Others (PLEASE SPECIFY)			
....	X	X	X
....	X	X	X

SUM

	21
	22
	23
	24
	25
	26
	27

ii　Which was the worst of these <u>mental</u> problems for YOU?

....

....

| | 28 |

iii　In what way has AA helped with the <u>mental</u> problems you
have experienced? ....

....

....

| | 29 |

E3　i　How many of the following social problems have you
experienced?　(PLEASE CIRCLE <u>ALL</u> PROBLEMS YOU HAVE HAD,
<u>AND</u> EACH PERIOD IN WHICH PERIOD YOU HAD THEM)

Social Problems	Experienced the problem:		
	Before <u>AA</u>	Since First <u>AA Meeting</u>	In Past <u>4 Weeks</u>
Had trouble with the police	1	2	4
Lost a job	1	2	4
Been in fights	1	2	4
Severe financial problems	1	2	4
Broken marriage	1	2	4
Neglected the family	1	2	4
Others (PLEASE SPECIFY)			
....	X	X	X
....	X	X	X

	30
	31
	32
	33
	34
	35
	36

Have you answered each question?　<u>PLEASE CHECK</u>

ii Which was the worst of these <u>social</u> problems for YOU?

....

....

iii In what ways has AA helped with the <u>social</u> problems

you have experienced? ....

....

....

....

38

SECTION F

<u>Your Contact With Professionals</u>

F1 Were you in contact with any professionals (such as G.P.'s

or Social Workers) during the period when drink was

causing you problems? (PLEASE CIRCLE TO SHOW ON CHART 2

WHICH PROFESSIONALS YOU WERE IN CONTACT WITH AND HOW

HELPFUL THEY WERE FOR YOUR PROBLEMS)

CHART 2

Professional	The Professional Was		
	Very Helpful	Fairly Helpful	Not Helpful At all
G.P.	1	2	3
Social Worker	1	2	3
Probation Officer	1	2	3
Psychiatrist	1	2	3
Clergyman/Priest	1	2	3
Other (PLEASE SPECIFY)			
....	X	X	X
....	X	X	X

☐ 39
☐ 40
☐ 41
☐ 42
☐ 43

☐ 44

<u>Have you answered each question?</u> <u>PLEASE CHECK</u>

F2 <u>Since you have been in AA</u> have you been in contact
with any professionals about drinking or drink-related
problems? (PLEASE CIRCLE TO SHOW ON CHART 3 WHICH
PROFESSIONALS YOU HAVE BEEN IN CONTACT WITH AND HOW HELPFUL
THEY WERE FOR YOUR PROBLEMS)

<u>CHART 3</u>

Professional	The Professional Was		
	Very Helpful	Fairly Helpful	Not Helpful At All
G.P.	1	2	3
Social Worker	1	2	3
Probation Officer	1	2	3
Psychiatrist	1	2	3
Clergyman/Priest	1	2	3
Other (PLEASE SPECIFY)			
....	X	X	X
....	X	X	X

45
46
47
48
49

50

F3 i Do you feel that AA has something to offer which no
professional can provide? (PLEASE CIRCLE)

                              NO   0
                              YES   X

    ii (IF YES) What is that? ....
        ....
        ....

51

<u>Have you answered each question?</u> PLEASE CHECK

SECTION C

Your General Comments on Aspects of A.A.

Gi What changes would you most like to see in the way

A.A. operates? ....

....

....

....

G2 i Do you think that A.A. could be more widely used as a
guide for groups of people with other kinds of problems?

(PLEASE CIRCLE)　　NO　1

YES　2

ii (IF YES) Which parts of the A.A. programme would
be particularly useful for other groups? ....

....

....

....

G3 Why do you think some people DON'T get on in A.A.? ....

....

....

....

FINALLY i What is your age? ....

ii What is your sex? (PLEASE CIRCLE)　Male　1

Female　2

Have you answered each question in the questionnaire?

PLEASE CHECK

REFERENCES

AA (undated) *Who Me?*, AA Publishing Co., London.

AA (undated) *Cooperation But Not Affiliation: How 'Alcoholics Anonymous' Cooperates with Outside Organisations within the Framework of AA Traditions*, World Services Inc., New York.

AA (1939) *Alcoholics Anonymous*, (1st ed.), Works Publishing Co., New York; (2nd ed., 1955), World Services Inc., New York.

AA (1940), *AA Bulletin*, No. 1, The Alcoholic Foundation, New York (mimeo).

AA (1952a), *44 Questions and Answers about the AA Program of Recovery from Alcoholism*, AA World Services Inc., New York.

AA (1952b), *Twelve Steps and Twelve Traditions*, AA World Services Inc., the AA Grapevine Inc., New York.

AA (1953), *This is AA*, World Services Inc., New York.

AA (1954), *The Alcoholic Wife: A Message to Husbands*, Alcoholics Anonymous Publishing Inc., New York.

AA (1955), *Alcoholics Anonymous and the Medical Profession*, AA World Services Inc., New York.

AA (1957), *Alcoholics Anonymous Comes of Age: A Brief History of AA*, World Services Inc., New York.

AA (1958), *Questions and Answers on Sponsorship*, AA World Services Inc., New York.

AA (1961), *Memo to an Inmate who may be an Alcoholic*, AA World Services Inc., New York.

AA (1965), *AA Fact File*, General Service Office, New York.

AA (1967), *The AA Way of Life*, AA World Services Inc., New York.

AA (1969), *The AA Service Manual*, World Services Inc., New York.

AA (1972a), *Alcoholics Anonymous: Findings of the United Kingdom Survey*, Mimeo, General Service Board, London.

AA (1972b), *AA World Directory*, Part II, AA World Services Inc., New York.

AA (1972c), *If You Are A Professional: AA Wants to Work With You*, General Services Inc., New York.

AA (1973), *Came to Believe*, AA World Services Inc., New York.

AA (1974), *AA Service Handbook for Great Britain*, General Service Board of AA (GB) Ltd., London.

AA (1975), *Box 514*, 1. 12.

AA (1977), *Annual Report of the General Service Board of Alcoholics Anonymous in Great Britain for the Year 1976.*

Alexander, J. (1941),'Alcoholics Anonymous', *Saturday Evening Post*, March 1.

Annals of the New York Academy of Sciences (1974), special edition on 'The Person with Alcoholism', editorial, 233.

Back, K.W. and Taylor, R.C. (1976), 'Self-Help Groups: Tool or Symbol', *J. Applied Behavioural Science*, 12. 295.

Bacon, S. (1957), 'A Sociologist Looks at AA', *Minnesota Welfare*, 10. 35.

Bales, R.F. (1945), 'Social Therapy for a Social Disorder — Compulsive Drinking', *J. Social Issues*, 1. 14.

Barish, H. (1971), 'Self-Help Groups', in *Encyclopaedia of Social Work, Vol. II*, National Association of Social Workers, New York, p. 1163.

Bean, M. (1975), 'Alcoholics Anonymous', *Psychiatric Annals*, 5. 20.

Bebbington, P.E. (1976), 'The Efficacy of Alcoholics Anonymous: the elusiveness of hard data', *Brit. J. Psychiat.*, 128. 572.

Bill W. (1949), 'The Society of Alcoholics Anonymous', *Amer. J. Psychiat.*, 106, 370.

Bill W. (1963), 'The Bill W. — Carl Jung Letters', *AA Grapevine*, 19. 8.

Bonacker, R. (1958), 'Alcoholism and Alcoholics Anonymous Viewed Symptomatologically', *Mental Hygiene*, 42. 562.

Brown, A. (1976), 'Big Problems for Little People', *Honey*, London, 10.

Brown, M.A. (1950), 'Alcoholic Profiles on the Minnesota Multiphasic', *J. Clin. Exp. Psychol.*, 9. 119.

Caplan, G. (1974), *Support Systems and Community Mental Health: Lectures on Concept Development*, New York.

Chafetz, M. and Demone, H. (1962), *Alcoholism and Society*, Oxford University Press, New York.

Chambers, Jnr., F. (1953), 'Analysis and Comparison of Three Treatment Measures for Alcoholism: Antabuse, the Alcoholics Anonymous Approach and Psychotherapy', *Brit. J. of Addictions*, 50. 29.

Clancy, J. (1964), 'Motivation Conflicts of the Alcohol Addict', *Quart. J. Stud. Alc.*, 25. 511.

Eddie (1975), 'My Source of Power', *Share: the Journal of AA in Great Britain*, 4. 37. 16.

Edwards, G. (1964), 'The Puzzle of AA', *New Society*, May 28.

Edwards, G., Hensman, C., Hawker, A., and Williamson, V. (1967), 'Alcoholics Anonymous the Anatomy of a Self-Help Group', *Social Psychiatry*, 1. 4.

Etzioni, A. (1964), *Modern Organizations*, Prentice-Hall, Englewood

Cliffs, New Jersey.

Gellman, I. (1964), *The Sober Alcoholic: An Organisation Analysis of Alcoholics Anonymous,* College and University Press, New Haven, Conn.

Gillie, O. (1975), 'Man, Help Thyself', *Sunday Times*, London, February 15.

Glatt, M.M. (1970), *The Alcoholic and the Help He Needs*, Priory Press, Herts.

Holmes, R. (1970), 'Alcoholics Anonymous as Group Logotherapy', *Pastoral Psychol.* 21–30.

Hurvitz, N.T. (1970), 'Peer Self-Help Psychotherapy Groups and their Implications for Psychotherapy', *Psychotherapy: Theory, Research and Practice*, 7. 1.

Ireland, Father John (1894), 'The Catholic Church and the Saloon', *North American Review*, LIX. 502.

Jackson, J.K. and Conner, R. (1953), 'The Skid Row Alcoholic', *Quart. J. Stud. Alc.,* 1. 468.

Jellinek, E.M. (1946), 'Phases in the Drinking History of Alcoholics: Analysis of a Survey Conducted by *Grapevine*, official organ of Alcoholics Anonymous, New York', *Quart. J. Stud. Alc.*, 7. 1.

Jellinek, E.M. (1960), *The Disease Concept of Alcoholism*, Hillhouse Press, New Haven, Conn.

Jertson, J. (1975), 'Self-Help Groups', *Social Work*, 20. 144.

Jones, R.K. (1970), 'Sectarian Characteristics of Alcoholics Anonymous', *Sociology*, 4. 181.

Katz, A. and Bender, E.I. (eds.) (1976), *The Strength in Us: Self-Help Groups in the Modern World*, Franklin Watts, New York.

Keller, M. (1960), 'The Definition of Alcoholism', *Quart. J. Stud. Alc.*, 21. 215.

Kessel, N. and Walton, H. (1965), *Alcoholism*, Penguin Books, Harmondsworth.

Killilea, M. (1976), 'Mutual Aid Organisations: Interpretations in the Literature' in Caplan, G. and Killilea, M. (eds.), *Support Systems and Mutual Help*, Grune Stratton, New York.

Kilmartin, A. (1973), *Understanding Cystitis*, Pan Books, London.

Kimberley, Lord (1976), 'Champagne from a tin mug on my crazy road to ruin', *Daily Mail*, London, January 16.

Kropotkin, P. (1944), *Mutual Aid*, Extending Horizon Books, Boston.

L.C. (1976), 'This Illness', *Share, The Journal of AA in Great Britain*, 4. 37. 3.

Leach, B. (1973), 'Does Alcoholics Anonymous Really Work?' in Bourne,

P. and Fox, R. (eds.), *Alcoholism: Progress in Research and Treatment*, Academic Press, New York.

Leach, B., Norris, J.L., Daucey, T. and Bissell, L. (1969), 'Dimensions of Alcoholics Anonymous: 1935–1965', *Int. J. Add.*, 4. 4. 507.

Madsen, W. (1974), 'Alcoholics Anonymous as a Crisis Cult', *Alcohol Health and Research World*, Spring, 2.

Maxwell, M. (1962), 'Alcoholics Anonymous: an Interpretation', in Pittman, D. and Snyder, C. (eds.), *Society, Culture and Drinking Patterns*, Wiley, New York.

McCann, J. (1976), 'AA Expects More Women Next Year', *The Journal*, 5. 12. 7.

McCarthy, R.G. (1946), 'Group Therapy in an Out-Patient Clinic for the Treatment of Alcoholism', *Quart. J. Stud. Alc.*, 7. 98.

MacKeith, N. (1975), 'Women Self-Help Groups', *Peace News*, 12. September 9.

Mowrer, O.H. (1961), *The Crisis in Psychiatry and Religion*, Van Nostrand, Princeton.

Mowrer, O.H. (1971), 'Peer Groups and Medication: the Best "Therapy" for Laymen and Professionals Alike', *Psychotherapy: Theory, Research and Practice*, 8. 44.

Mowrer, O.H. (1976), 'The "Self-Help" or Mutual Aid Movement: Do Professionals Help or Hinder?', *Self-Help and Health: A Report*, New Human Sciences Institute, New York.

Newell, K.N. (ed.) (1975), *Health By The People*, World Health Organisation, Geneva.

Norris, J.L. (1974), *Alcoholics Anonymous 1974 Members Survey*, AA World Services Inc., New York.

Norris, J.L. (1976), quoted in McCann, J., 'AA Expects more Women Next Year', *The Journal*, 5. 12. 7.

Powell, T.J. (1975), 'The Use of Self-Help Groups as Supportive Reference Communities', *American Journal of Orthopsychiatry*, 45. 756.

Ritchie, O. (1948), 'A Socio-historical Survey of Alcoholics Anonymous', *Quart. J. Stud. Alc.*, 9. 119.

Robinson, D. (1976), *From Drinking to Alcoholism: A Sociological Commentary*, John Wiley, London.

Robinson, D. and Henry, S. (1977), *Self-Help and Health: Mutual Aid for Modern Problems*, Martin Robertson, London.

Seiberling, H. (1971), 'Message to the Akron AA Group's Founder's Day Meeting', (Mimeo).

Seixas, F. and Cadaret, R. (1974), 'Alcoholics Anonymous and

Beyond', *Ann. New York Acad. Sci.*, 233. 135.

Stewart, D. (1955), 'The Dynamics of Fellowship Illustrated in Alcoholics Anonymous', *Quart J. Stud. Alc.*, 16. 251.

Thune, P. (1977), 'Alcoholism and the Archetypal Past: A Phenomenological Perspective on Alcoholics Anonymous', *Journal of Studies on Alcohol*, 38. 1. 75.

Tiebout, H.M. (1944), 'Therapeutic Mechanisms of Alcoholics Anonymous', *Amer. J. of Psychiat.*, 468.

Tiebout, H. (1961), 'Alcoholics Anonymous – an Experiment of Nature', *Quart. J. Stud. Alc.*, 22. 52.

Toch, H. (1965), *The Social Psychology of Social Movements*, Bobbs-Merrill, Illinois.

Traunstein, D.M. and Steinman, R. (1973), 'Voluntary Self-Help Organisations: An Exploratory Study', *Journal of Voluntary Action Research*, 2. 230.

Trice, H.M. (1957), 'A Study of the Process of Affiliation with Alcoholics Anonymous', *Quart. J. Stud. Alc.* 18. 39.

Trice, H.M. (1958), 'Alcoholics Anonymous', *Ann. Amer. Acad. Polit. Soc. Sci.*, CCCXV. 108.

Trice, H.M. (1959), 'The Affiliation Motive and Readiness to Join Alcoholics Anonymous', *Quart. J. Stud. Alc.*, 20. 313.

Trice, H. and Roman, P. (1970), 'Delabelling and Relabelling and Alcoholics Anonymous', *Social Problems*, 17. 538.

Vattano, A. (1972), 'Power to the People: Self-Help Groups', *Social Work*, 17. 7.

Wilson, R. (1951), 'An Evaluation of Treatment Methods in Alcoholism Therapy', *Mental Hygiene*, 35. 260.

Wootton, A. (1977), 'Sharing: Some Notes on the Organisation of Talk in a Therapeutic Community', *Sociology*, 11.

AUTHOR INDEX

149

SUBJECT INDEX

AA: and conventional help 106–11; and the medical profession 80–1, 106–11, 117–18; as a model for self-help groups 11; as a social movement 34; as a sub-culture 34–5; as a way of life 12, 35–6, 94–116; as self-help group 9–10, 36; *Grapevine* 16, 23; in Great Britain 18–19; literature 83–6

Abstinence and sobriety 105–6, 118–19
Action in self-help groups 76–7
Admitting the problem 61–2
Affiliation 37–9, 119
Akron, Ohio 12, 15, 16, 17
Alcoholics Anonymous Comes of Age 15, 17, 84, 101
Alcoholics Anonymous ('The Big Book') 15, 16, 20, 45, 66, 84, 85, 92, 101
Alcoholism as an allergy 30–1
Alcoholism as the problem 56–61, 118; AA's definition of 59–60; defining 57–8; general public's definition 61
Anti-professionalism 14
Attendance of meetings 46–7, 51–2, 82–3

Becoming a member 12, 37–54
Being an alcoholic for ever 62–3, 119
Box 514 55, 63, 85, 92
Breakthrough Trust 81

CARE (Cancer Aftercare and Rehabilitation Society) 74
Causes of alcoholism 30–1
Changes in AA 111–16; desire for 111–16; in relation to meetings 111–12; in relation to publicity 113–16
Characteristics of self-help groups 76
Cleveland, Ohio 23
Collection at meetings 25, 49
Conferences 24, 87
Continuity of help 106–11; and separation 106–7
Conventions 87
Coping through involvement 12, 76–93

Decline of supporting institutions 14
Deconstructing the problem 56, 61–3, 82
Disillusionment with existing services 14
Division of labour 21, 22
Drop-outs 52–4; and sponsorship 92–3

Financial independence 25–56
First meeting 46–50; unacceptability of 53–4
Friendship 94–100; and AA 97; and cliques 98; and relationships 96; development of 99–100; value of 99

Gamblers Anonymous 11, 106
General Service Board 22, 52, 111
General Service Conference 24, 87
General Service Office 8
Gingerbread 11
Groups: autonomy of 24; size of 72; splitting 72–3; with different purposes 73
Growth of AA 17–20

Handling the drinking experience 67
History of AA 9, 12, 15–21

Identification 12, 44–6, 50–1, 53, 55, 65, 68–9, 74–5, 118
Intergroups 24
Interpretations of AA 31–5
Involvement in AA activities 12, 82–93
Involvement in social activities 12, 94–100; importance of 96; opportunities for 95–6

Knowledge of AA 43

Lone members 17

151